Polyphonic Writing
for Voices

To my friend Herbert Howells

Polyphonic Writing
for Voices

IN SIX AND EIGHT PARTS

By

GEORGE OLDROYD

OXFORD UNIVERSITY PRESS

LONDON   NEW YORK   TORONTO

OXFORD UNIVERSITY PRESS
(*Music Department*)
44 CONDUIT STREET, LONDON, W. I
GEOFFREY CUMBERLEGE
PUBLISHER TO THE UNIVERSITY

PRINTED LITHOGRAPHICALLY IN GREAT BRITAIN
AT THE UNIVERSITY PRESS, OXFORD
BY CHARLES BATEY, PRINTER TO THE UNIVERSITY

CONTENTS

5

The function of the Leading-note originally and in later times. The loss of colour-strength of the leading-note under the major and minor key system. The perfect cadence the ordinary effect; no longer novel. The freedom of the leading-note in a melodic curve (often falls though the harmony changes); the leading-note present in both choirs; omitted in one choir and doubled in the other. Double-choir writing virtually the same as eight-part writing.

CONTENTS

ACKNOWLEDGEMENTS

THE PUBLISHERS wish to express their thanks to Professor Arthur Hutchings for his help in preparing this book for publication.

Thanks are also due to the following publishers for permission to quote extracts from works in their catalogues:

Messrs. Augener Ltd.	J. A. WESTRUP: *When Israel came out of Egypt.*
Messrs. A. & C. Black Ltd.	CHARLES WOOD: *Haec Dies*; *Hail Gladdening Light*; *Magnificat and Nunc Dimittis in E major* (double choir); *Magnificat and Nunc Dimittis (Collegium Regale).*
Messrs. Boosey & Hawkes Ltd.	PETER WARLOCK: *As Dew in Aprylle.* GORDON JACOB: *To Music to becalm his fever.*
Messrs. Chappell & Co. Ltd.	ARNOLD BAX: *Ora Mater Filium*
The Clarendon Press, Oxford.	C. H. KITSON: *Evolution of Harmony.*
Messrs. J. Curwen & Sons Ltd.	GUSTAV HOLST: *The Evening Watch.* E. W. NAYLOR: *Magnificat and Nunc Dimittis.* R. VAUGHAN WILLIAMS: *Mass in G Minor.*
Messrs. G. T. Foulis & Co. Ltd.	BURNEY: *A General History of Music*, Vol. II.
Messrs. Macmillan & Co. Ltd.	R. O. MORRIS: *Foundations of Practical Harmony.*
Messrs. Novello & Co. Ltd.	CHARLES MACPHERSON: *Communion Service in E flat.* HUBERT PARRY: *Blest Pair of Sirens*; *Sorrow and Pain.* C. V. STANFORD: *Te Deum in B flat.*
The Oxford University Press.	E. H. FELLOWES: *The English Madrigal Composers.* W. G. WHITTAKER: *Collected Essays.* R. VAUGHAN WILLIAMS: *Down Ampney.*
Messrs. Stainer & Bell, Ltd.	HERBERT HOWELLS: *A Spotless Rose*; *Here is the little door.* C. V. STANFORD: *Ye Holy Angels Bright.* THOMAS WOOD: *Chanticlier.*

INTRODUCTION

IT is not the purpose of this book to give specific attention to the idiosyncrasies of Palestrina, Byrd, and other writers of the sixteenth century, whose works must be studied in great detail if we are to gather from them a true understanding of the attitude of these composers regarding contrapuntal technique; rather, it is intended to give a general survey of writing for voices, particularly in six and eight parts, for those desirous of gaining experience in such work; and with this in mind, guidance has been sought from the works of composers recognized for their contribution to this branch of musical literature.

Technical skill is the *sine qua non* of musical composition, which is often referred to as *free* composition, implying that the composer has *complete* freedom. Surely it should be freedom springing from clear understanding and mastery of technique; not the kind of thing 'picked up as you go along', as a student called it. Academic study is a preparation for this—a training-ground for the acquisition of technical ability—without which a student is not likely to go far. If it cannot give inspiration it can at least instil an appreciation of the value of *order*, which is the first essential.

A period of apprenticeship is a necessity, during which the student learns to handle and make the most of his tools. It is a fascinating experience; it may at times be humbling; it certainly demands patience. The designing and carving of intertwining stems and tendrils in a Grinling Gibbons panel have their counterpart in the musician's art. Gibbons had first to develop skill before he could create beauty; and he had to work for it. It is equally true of the composer, and indeed we know that Bach, Haydn, and Mozart were not ashamed to acknowledge how hard they worked and practised to gain their skill. They did not just 'pick it up'.

Although in these pages we are concerned with technique, yet that is not all that concerns the creative musician. It may be the first thing, but it is certainly not the last; for he may possess enviable craftsmanship, and yet create nothing of great worth. The *quality* of his own mind plays its part.

Examination problems test the technique and musicianship of the student. He should so use the voices as to show knowledge of their expressive powers, placing them so that their contribution is most effective, just as in orchestration. Were not Palestrina and Byrd masters of *vocal* orchestration? The student should dispose the voices so that they mingle well together, balancing their tone and blending their colours. Never should he lose sight of the flow and sweep of the individual parts, remembering that ugly lines spoil vocal polyphony just as they mar a picture or piece of sculpture. The finest texture is made of beautifully curving strands of tone, moving in harmonious relationship.

Here and there will be found passing reference to four-part writing. Such examples as 15, 15*a*, 15*b* (p. 19) may be eye-openers to many; but they show the mind of the mature musician, and the principles they stand for should be part and parcel of good technique. It is our duty to grasp the purpose behind them and make use of it, for it is simply musical common sense.

The suggestions in the first six chapters extend, and even sometimes contradict, the rules of six- and eight-part vocal writing hitherto laid down; but they are substantiated by the fact that the usages they bring to our notice have been the common practice of a long line of distinguished musicians, and therefore should be incorporated into the student's normal equipment. In examination problems the student is at liberty to show freedom in his work; but he should do so convincingly.

In Chapter VII are offered some conclusions drawn from observations concerning the use of direct and close consecutive octaves and fifths. By the latter is meant consecutives occurring on the weak parts of consecutive beats, or separated by a short rest.

Parry's *Blest Pair of Sirens* has for a long time been recommended to students as a fine example of eight-part writing. It is thoroughly English, and no doubt was regarded as good straightforward stuff of exactly the right kind for them. On close examination, however, it will be found to contain things that are not at all 'just straightforward' from a technical point of view. It brings us face to face with consecutives in circumstances which demand careful scrutiny. The student would be inclined to use his blue pencil without hesitation, and no doubt with much delight; but it may be taken for granted that Parry was fully aware of how he wrote, and winked at nothing. These are among the matters treated in this seventh chapter.

The closing chapter, the eighth, continues the explorations in Chapter VII. Interesting points in the matter of discord caused by bold lines in both simple and complex scores are brought forward. It will be seen what Henry Purcell conceived as good legitimate writing in this respect, and how modern composers have followed on.

There are, too, effects which may be classed under the heading of vocal orchestration, as when a note or two in one voice may be underlined in another.

Some composers use consecutive fifths in ecclesiastical writing to create an atmosphere which no other means can yield. Examples are provided for consideration; such consecutives may occur as a single pair here and there, or more continuously.

Furthermore, there are aspects of the occurrence of *occasional* consecutive fifths, particularly in a many-part score, which have often aroused my curiosity and given rise to reflections which I venture to express. We all know that to experienced composers the problem of consecutive fifths is an aesthetic, not a grammatical one; and after all it is from them that we learn. A quiet double pedal (root and fifth) creates a velvety depth of sound over which voices may mingle with special effect; an occasional pair of fifths, particularly between the two lowest voices of a many-part score, produces a similar quality of tone for the passing moment. This is of musical value, as it adds to the variety of tone-character and, like a brief discord, makes an acceptable contribution to expressiveness. Why, therefore, regard such writing as an offence? Such occurrences need not be attributed to faulty technique, or associated with the pedestrian writing of a plodder; for they demand the mature judgement of the composer's artistic mind. They are likely to come about by the composer's making the most of any opportunity to improve the curve and expressive power of the voice parts. They are due not to a lack of skill or experience, but to a sensitive awareness of their effect. Organ builders long ago knew the value of mutation stops [quint, &c.], which serve to *bind together* the web of sounds of the full organ and give richness. The occasional fifths of which I write may serve in some degree the same purpose of binding together and enriching the many strands of singing-tone; they do, in fact, create a *natural* sonority.

The relaxations by which composers have extended vocal technique and expression are here approached with an open mind, with the purpose of discovering musical reason behind what at first sight might appear to be tactics of convenience. If they were originally tactics of convenience, they have undoubtedly become recognized tools of musical craftsmanship. It is hoped that advanced students may derive something helpful to their own creative work from the comments made upon such relaxations.

The musical examples are, in the main, taken from religious vocal music, but they illustrate points which are common to secular writing also.

The COURSE OF STUDY is divided into two main parts covering sixteenth-century and later styles. Opportunity is provided for becoming conversant in some degree with the accepted characteristics of polyphonic writing. This experience should prepare the ground for deeper and specialized study, for it will be clear to those who read this short book that it merely opens the door upon an extensive and engrossing sphere of musical art.

CHAPTER I

Sixteenth-century and Later Styles of Writing

THE NECESSITY FOR RELAXATION OF GENERALLY ACCEPTED
RULES OF FOUR-PART WRITING WHEN APPLIED TO SIX-
AND EIGHT-PART WORK.
INDEFINITENESS OF RULES.
WHY ANY RESTRICTION UPON DOING AS THE GREAT
MASTERS DID?

MODERN unaccompanied vocal composition is a combination of harmonic and contrapuntal thought.

In sixteenth-century art the manner of writing was mainly contrapuntal: there was much display of an imitative kind. There were also patches of chordal writing which served as offsets to the imitative. Nevertheless, the general build-up of a composition was a series of spans or periods in which imitation played a great part. The 'Kyrie', 'Sanctus', 'Agnus Dei' in Palestrina's Mass *Aeterna munera Christi* illustrate this perfectly. The *harmonic result* of the combination of these imitative voice parts was simple, but had a character quite its own, owing to the modal derivation of the melodic phrases. The harmonic potentialities of our major and minor scales were unrecognized though increasingly used.

Modern work may be conceived on similar lines to the above, though imbued with modern colour. It may also spring from an attitude of mind fundamentally harmonic, creating longer flights of melody which call, not for imitative treatment, but for harmonization by additional parts. The contrapuntal skill which wove the imitative phrases into a delightful musical texture in sixteenth-century writing is indeed just as necessary in adding parts to a modern expansive melody. These added parts, though not imitating the chief melody, must combine to make good musical texture. Compare any harmonization of the Chorale 'Inns-bruck' by Bach with, say, Sullivan's tune 'St. Gertrude', sung to 'Onward, Christian Soldiers'. In the former each voice has melodic curve and flow in a manner which is not present in the latter. These features—melodic contour and rhythmic interest—are characteristics of good contrapuntal writing, and should be evident in the treatment of modern vocal composition *even though its basis is harmonic*.

Thus we see two broad styles:

1. A sixteenth-century style distinguished by phrase-imitation, by flow and curve of vocal line, and by integrity of texture.

2. A modern style which harmonizes a chief melodic line by the addition of
other lines, not necessarily imitative, but not devoid of linear interest.

Just as chordal patches served as relief from the imitative periods in sixteenth-century work, so in modern composition imitation may serve the purpose of contrast with the harmonic writing. Further, in modern composition the scope for harmonic colour and imagination knows no bounds other than practical suitability for the voices.

These observations seem almost too simple to bring to the notice of the student; but too often does he show misunderstanding of what a problem calls for, and so uses his tools wrongly. He confuses a contrapuntal problem with a harmonic one, and wrecks a question calling for harmonic treatment by trying to work it contrapuntally. He imagines that *imitation* is the infallible clue to success, no matter how injurious to harmony: he fails to recognize that there is ample virtue in attractively flowing parts. Surely half the battle in working a problem is in recognizing what the question calls for; confidence that it is being rightly tackled settles the mind. Sense of style can assist in this matter.

In six-part and eight-part writing it is not enough to have avoided grammatical pitfalls. If the student puts himself in the place of a member of a choir which may perform what he writes, he will need no urging to distribute the interest, for this simply means that *all* the singers have something worth singing.

To look at the score of a fine piece of vocal writing is a pleasure; it all appears so natural and effortless and as though it could not be different. To watch a first class golfer is also a joy; his movements are so easy, his shots are sure; in a word, his technique fulfils his desire. So must it be with the musician: his technique must be such as will respond to his inspiration.

It has always been recognized that the rules of four-part writing cannot be applied to six- and eight-part work without relaxation. The trouble is that guidance about this relaxation by theorists appears to be vague. For instance, Fux assures his pupil that, having mastered four-part composition, his way is already clear about writing for more voices, for, as the number of voices increases, the rules are to be less rigorously observed. Students have heard this last sentence numberless times, with its tantalizing lack of precise information. Students will tell you that they never seem lucky enough to use the right relaxation at the right moment.

However that may be, it cannot be said that Macfarren was vague, no matter how drastic he was in the rules he laid down in his book on Counterpoint published in 1887. It should not be overlooked that Macfarren, as Professor of Music in the University of Cambridge and Principal of the Royal Academy of Music, wielded both power and influence. In his book the following statements are to be found concerning counterpoint in six or more parts:

13

'Progression from 1st to 8th, or from 8th to 1st, or from 8th to 8th by contrary motion is allowable; not so 5th to 5th.

Any note of a chord may be doubled except it be the leading note; but the use of this must be as exclusively restricted to one single part, as in two-part harmony. It is still imperative that no part cross another, except only when the shorter notes of one part proceed above or below a longer note that is sustained against them.'

The above is quoted merely as indicative of the state of things which prevailed towards the end of the nineteenth century. Musically it condemns itself. Need we linger over Macfarren?

Another author—Prout—considers that no new rules are needed for writing in more than four parts, and the practice of the best composers will be clearly understood by the study of examples which he provides. These are limited to two examples in five parts from Bach and Mendelssohn; two in six parts from Handel and Brahms; one in seven parts by Handel; and two in eight parts from Cherubini and Mendelssohn. He observes that examples of a doubled leading-note occur, *even* in the works of the great masters, but suggests that it is better avoided if possible.

But why the restriction upon doing as the great masters did? Why trouble to find out how they wrote, and then warn students against doing the same? Surely it is only by observing how the masters handled their material and by realizing why they did so that the student develops his own sense and power of style. Students should sit at the feet of the artist, not of the pedant.

CHAPTER II

The Leading-note

I. IN SIX-PART WRITING

SINCE no specific mention is made in current textbooks of the doubled leading-note in six-part work, students may find that the following examples give them helpful guidance. They are from Richard Dering (d. 1630), a musician of high repute; Handel; and the late Charles Wood.

[Ex. 3 from Handel shows at ⊕ the two basses joining forces. This kind of thing is quite common in many-part writing.]

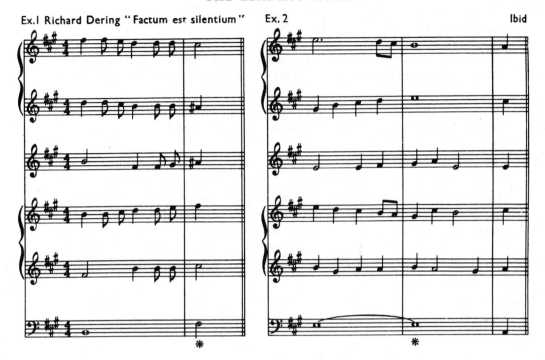

Ex.1 Richard Dering "Factum est silentium" Ex. 2 Ibid

Ex.3 Handel "The King shall rejoice" Ex.4 Charles Wood "Haec dies"

CONCLUSION

These examples furnish evidence that the leading-note may be doubled in six-part writing.

Nevertheless, this should not be done indiscriminately: melodic line, harmonic balance in the disposition of the parts, must always control the situation. In the examples from Dering and Wood we see melodic line dictating the usage which the theorists have eschewed; and in the example from Handel we see harmonic balance leading to a similar infraction of 'rules'.

II. IN DOUBLE-CHOIR WRITING AND EIGHT-PART WRITING

The late Dr. Kitson, who went into some detail about rules, asserted that, although the leading-note may be doubled, such doubling is objectionable *if one occurrence* of the leading-note is in the bass. He is referring to eight-part choir and double-choir writing.

It is found that Parry, Mendelssohn, Purcell, and Bach indulged freely in the doubling of the leading-note. Bach *doubles it in the bass* at the octave, that is, in the first and second bass parts. He even *trebles* the leading-note, in which case it occurs twice in the same choir in double-choir work, at the unison, too.

Here are examples from several sources:

Ex. 5   Parry "Blest Pair of Sirens" page 11, bar 6.

Ex. 6   Mendelssohn "114th Psalm" page 5, bar 7

Ex. 7   Bach "The Spirit also helpeth us" Double Choir   page 5

Ex. 8   Idem, page 9 Double Choir

CONCLUSION

The above examples are evidence:

(*a*) that the leading-note may be doubled, nay, trebled, in eight-part and double-choir writing, even when it occurs in the bass;

(*b*) that in double-choir work it may be doubled in the same choir.
Such treatment, however, should not be indiscriminate: the part-movement and
disposition of the harmony should justify it.

CHAPTER III

Consecutive Octaves and Fifths by Contrary Motion

IN this matter, again, we find unwarrantable restrictions laid down by the
theoretical writers. One says that consecutive fifths and octaves by contrary
motion may be used freely, not differentiating between six-part and eight-part
writing. Another insists that in *six parts* consecutive octaves may be taken by
contrary motion; whereas in *seven and eight parts*, though consecutive fifths are
admissible, they should not precede or follow consecutive octaves between the
same two parts.

I. Let us consider what the great masters teach us by example about SIX-PART
writing

Here are excerpts from Byrd's Anthem 'Sing joyfully unto God':

The following, from Tallis's 'If ye love me', shows that octaves by contrary motion were not *forbidden* even in four-part harmony when a good purpose was being served:

Bach, in his four-part chorales, does not scruple to indulge in the same kind of thing:

Nor indeed does R. Vaughan Williams, witness his hymn-tune, 'Down Ampney':

The following is from Gibbons's 'Hosanna to the Son of David':

Parry's 'Sorrow and Pain' shows the following, where are seen consecutive octaves and fifths on two successive *main* beats; although the part-movements, reckoned from the second quaver (marked *) of the first main beat to the next, are normal. They are mentioned because they are the kind of thing which is apt to bother a student. Although the slow tempo might be regarded as a mitigating circumstance, we are justified in inferring from the example that Parry had no qualms about the effect.

Ex. 17   Parry " Sorrow and pain "

Richard Dering in his Motet 'Cantate Domino' writes:

Ex. 18

CONCLUSION

These examples provide evidence that indulgence in consecutive octaves and fifths by contrary motion has been common practice.

If composers of such prominence found no reason to avoid them, why should they be prohibited to students, rightly guided?

II. Let us now consider EIGHT-PART writing

(a) *Eight-part score*, that is, single eight-part choir.

There is such abundant proof that consecutive octaves and fifths in contrary motion have always been recognized in the technique of eight-part writing in score, that it is not essential to provide examples. One author restricts this kind of thing to 'not more than two moves', but there is no warrant for this ruling in the usage of the great composers.

(b) *Double-choir* (that is, double four-part choir).

Observations here below show that Palestrina did not scruple to use consecutive octaves and fifths by contrary motion far beyond two moves, when only the bass parts were involved.

His *Stabat Mater* shows a string of consecutive octaves by contrary motion between the bass parts of the two choirs:

Ex. 19

This example is *virtually* seven-part writing.

There seems no reason why this string of consecutive octaves should not be permissible in single eight-part choir writing. Two choirs, separated as they are by the arrangement of the choir stalls in cathedrals, are so placed for antiphonal singing. It is a perfect arrangement. When, however, both choirs join forces and produce eight strands of tone mingling together, the effect is virtually the same no matter whether the singers are arranged as a double four-part choir or as a single choir composed of eight strands of tone. If, after a Nunc Dimittis for double four-part choir, an eight-part anthem were performed—as might well happen—the singers would not walk about the chancel and alter their positions on that account. Obviously then, as far as the listener is concerned, the effect is the same, no matter whether the music is *written down* in the double-choir style or the eight-strand style.

21

Therefore, with regard to a chain of consecutive octaves between two bass parts in contrary motion, the ruling must be the same for writing in double four-part choir as for an eight-strand choir.

CONCLUSION

It may be said that consecutive octaves and fifths by contrary motion have been a general practice.

It is evident that consecutive octaves by contrary motion between two bass parts have been commonly used for *a number of moves*, and are valid for writing in either double four-part score or eight-part score. Nevertheless, if continued for more than a few moves, the writing no longer remains eight-part. For this reason it should be avoided in a test specifically demanding eight real parts.

It was noted that Example No. 19 is virtually seven-part writing : the two basses sing the same notes, alternately at the unison and octave. Frequently enough the same effect occurs, but in balder fashion, when the two bass parts duplicate each other either at the octave or unison. Example No. 20 is an illustration :

Ex. 20   Bach "Sing ye to the Lord"

CHAPTER IV

The Treatment of the Dominant Seventh Chord and Secondary Seventh Chords

THE DOMINANT SEVENTH CHORD

ONE author states that Fundamental Discords should not be doubled as a rule; but gives two exceptions to this generalization:

    (*a*) When a discord is capable of two resolutions, one part may take one resolution, another the alternative (see Ex. 21);

    (*b*) or, one part may descend to another note of the same harmony (see Ex. 22).

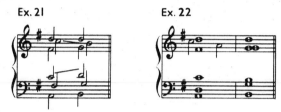

Ex. 21   Ex. 22

But such doubling (he adds) would be poor if one of the discords moved irregularly, e.g.:

Ex. 23

'Such things may be seen,' the author continues, 'but the mental effect of the part is bad. As a matter of fact such doubling is hardly even necessary, and the student should aim at its avoidance rather than its use.'

The above suggestions commend themselves as *first* considerations. Composers often carry out the normal double treatment of a discordant note capable of two resolutions; but *they do not hesitate to do otherwise* and indulge in what our author would call irregular treatments (Ex. 23).

It will be remembered that according to textbook rule, the seventh of the dominant seventh chord may rise only when the chord is in the second inversion and is followed by the tonic chord in the first inversion. Obviously, therefore, in eight-part work it is reasonable to take advantage of this and double the seventh note, allowing one to rise and the other to fall (Ex. 22). Parry evidently considered that this treatment should also apply when the dominant seventh chord was in the root position, as the following examples show:

Ex. 24   Parry "Blest Pair of Sirens"   Ex. 25   Ibid

Note also, in Ex. 24, the consecutive fifths between first alto and second bass (see Chapter VII, pp. 50 et seq.).

Parry had no hesitation in indulging in treatment of the doubled seventh note far more *irregular* than anything quoted by certain authors. Ex. 25 is a striking instance. This undoubtedly reveals the mind of Parry. The melodic fall of the first soprano part was felt so powerfully that no *rules* were allowed to interfere with it. *This is the true spirit of counterpoint*; it is the *melodic* spirit which asserts that the *bent* of a melody—I would call it the *magnetic pull*—is so strong that rules of harmonic part-movement break down. It is clear that there is much musical wisdom to be gleaned from Parry.

The next example, from Mendelssohn's 114th Psalm, provides another 'irregular' treatment of the doubled seventh. Here, one of the sevenths rises by step and the other by leap.

Ex. 26

In both these moves there is no practical difficulty to the singers. It is a matter of interest, however, to note that the second soprano and second alto at this point proceed in consecutive *seconds*, a tone apart.[1] It would be worth the student's while to consider if this arrangement could be improved. No doubt Mendelssohn thought over it carefully and decided to leave it. That happened, of course, long before textbooks dealt extensively with the intricacies of eight-part writing.

Bach, in Ex. 27 from Motet No. 2, 'The Spirit also helpeth us', shows the chord of the dominant seventh in the last inversion with the discordant seventh

---

[1] Consecutive *sevenths* and *ninths* are quite common, as can be seen in the following excerpts from chorales by Bach:

Ex. 26(a)   Ex. 26 (b)

doubled in the highest soprano voice. Thus the seventh appears in the extreme parts! The great master appears to avoid consecutive octaves between these two outer parts by the expedient of allowing the upper one to be prolonged as a suspension, thus delaying its resolution, whilst the lower part resolves immediately.

Ex. 27

Ex. 27 is an interesting case which shows that it would never have done for composers to wait for the theorists' acquiescence before daring to get on with their job. It may surprise us to discover that Tallis, 150 years earlier, avoided consecutive octaves in a manner comparable to the above by Bach. One wonders if Tallis ever thought there was *need* to avoid them; it was surely rather a matter of *using* such things as one of his sharper tools. Further comment upon this will be found on pp. 53 and 65–6. Even the few bars quoted from Bach in Ex. 27 bristle with processes which will lead the keen student to browse over the rest of the Motet.

CONCLUSION

It is clear that the seventh of the dominant seventh chord may be doubled and given the twofold resolution (usually associated with the chord in its second inversion) even though the chord is in *root position* or *any inversion*.

Further, the seventh may be doubled, and in one instance resolved, while in the other it is treated irregularly; that is, not by step. This treatment seems available so long as the part concerned can *readily be felt and taken by the singer*. This is the final criterion, and seems to have been so ever since the art of vocal composition began to develop. If a discord like the seventh is doubled and this doubling does not spoil the balance harmonically, then it must, at the composer's desire, yield to irregular treatment. Such treatment is finally settled by its practical suitability to the singer. What was impossible in the days of Palestrina may be quite simple to singers of our own times; such is the way of progress. What was once regarded as *irregular* becomes *regular*; were this not so we could never have had the B Minor Mass and other great works.

I would draw the reader's attention to what I have called *magnetic pull* in a melodic curve: I believe it to be of far-reaching importance in its bearing upon melodic suppleness, grace, and expressiveness. It is by no means a modern force, for it springs from Plainsong in which it appears to be inherent. It is seen and realized in a well-known figure used by all sixteenth-century composers and even earlier ones. This figure has a discordant note quitted by leap and not always resolved according to our conceptions of resolution. Here are examples of it (*a*), (*b*), (*c*), (*d*):

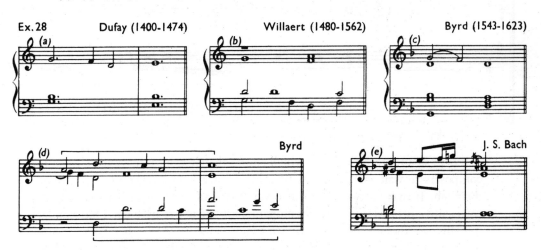

The same idea is evident in the works of later composers. The quotation (*e*), above, is an interesting instance from Bach.

SECONDARY SEVENTH CHORDS (diatonic sevenths)

Authors of some textbooks state that in diatonic seventh chords the seventh should not be doubled unless remaining to be a part of the next chord. As illustrating this, the following is provided:

Ex. 29

Again it must be said that if composers had been governed by the above simple rule much fine music would never have been created.

Consider Bach's harmonization of 'Liebster Immanuel', from which the last few chords are quoted:

Ex. 30

At the asterisk is, plainly enough, a chord of the seventh, with the seventh note, D, doubled. There can be no quibbling about this, for Bach could have written B instead of D in the soprano, or an E minim in the tenor. It may be said without hesitation that Bach's choice sprang from contrapuntal rather than harmonic interest; and, further, that Bach felt a strong magnetic pull from D to A sharp. This interval arrests the attention and has an emotional appeal; there is all the difference in this respect between the interval C sharp down to A sharp on the one hand, and D down to A sharp on the other. Here, as in the cases previously mentioned (Ex. 28), we see a grammatical irregularity caused by the magnetic pull of the musical curve.

The following is from E. W. Naylor's *Magnificat and Nunc Dimittis in A major* for double-choir.

Ex. 31

Here is the chord of the submediant seventh in *root position* with the seventh note doubled (1) (1). The seventh in the second soprano part falls by step, and in the first tenor rises by step. In passing, note the consecutive fifths between the second alto and first tenor (2) (2), and the consecutive octaves between first tenor and second bass (3) (3).

Mendelssohn's 114th Psalm, Ex. 32, shows the supertonic seventh chord in *root position* with the seventh note occurring in both the alto parts. One remains and the other leaps.

Ex. 32

In Ex. 33, from Parry's *Blest Pair of Sirens*, although the seventh of the supertonic seventh chord is not doubled, yet it is worth noting that the root A and the seventh G move to the same note, F sharp, by contrary motion. This movement of parts is often queried by students.

In Ex. 33 *a*, from the same work by Parry, we observe the supertonic seventh chord in the first inversion, with the seventh note occurring twice. In the first alto it falls by step; in the first tenor it falls by a fourth.

Ex. 33   Ex. 33 *(a)*

Ex. 33 *b,* from Charles Wood's 'Hail, gladdening Light', provides us with an instance in which the seventh is quitted by leap in both the first alto and second tenor; but the singers can readily feel their notes.

Ex. 33 *(b)*

In Gordon Jacob's work, 'To Music to becalm his fever', Ex. 34, is seen a supertonic seventh chord in the first inversion at the second crotchet beat. The seventh note, C, is doubled in the first treble and first alto parts; the one remains to be a suspension, the other leaps.

Ex. 34

CONCLUSION

The above examples indicate clearly that the seventh note in secondary seventh chords need not be restricted to one part. When the seventh note is doubled, the following treatments, at least, are possible:

1. Both may remain to be a part of the next chord.
2. One may remain and the other leap.
3. One may rise by step and the other fall by step.
4. One may fall by step and the other fall by leap.
5. One may rise by leap and the other fall by leap.
6. One may remain as a suspension and the other leap.
7. Both may leap.

That such freedom of the discordant seventh as we have seen should occur in eight-part composition is not surprising. What may be surprising is to find it occurring in four-part composition. We have, however, already seen it in Bach, and it is to be seen in Stanford. Furthermore, the example by Stanford in his *Te Deum in B flat* is closely akin to that of Bach, Ex. 30, for it demonstrates the influence of magnetic pull in the melody. If a melody had a strong bent towards a certain point, that was deemed, by Stanford, sufficient justification for him to remove obstacles. Here are the last four bars from his *Te Deum*:

Ex. 35

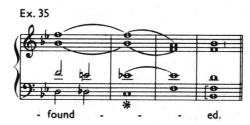

- found - - - ed.

The chord at the asterisk is the second inversion of the dominant seventh with the leading-note delayed, the B flat being a suspension though not resolving in the same voice part. Had the soprano voice crossed the alto by taking the octave leap down to the low F, and had the alto passed on to the leading-note, A, there would have been no grammatical irregularity. Why did Stanford not write it in that fashion? I venture to suggest that he felt the movement of the parts *as written* in his score. The resolution of the suspension is taken over by the magnetic pull of the soprano part down from F to A. The melody had a strong bent from F down towards A, and Stanford allowed nothing to interfere with it. I have never heard of singers experiencing any difficulty in performing their parts, and, no doubt, most of them have been quite unaware of any grammatical irregularity at that point.

31

CHAPTER V

The Treatment of the Added Sixth Chord
and the Augmented Sixth Chords

THE ADDED SIXTH CHORD

WHEN the added sixth chord moves to the tonic chord, the sixth in the chord seems naturally to step away from the fifth and pass to the third of the tonic. Kitson considered that, although any note of this added sixth chord could be doubled, it is better not to double the sixth, as is seen in the following example:

Ex. 36

Here it was considered that the note D, rather than C, is discordant.

In Ex. 37, from Parry's *Blest Pair of Sirens*, we see the normal treatment as shown in Ex. 36; but it should be noted that the spacing of the last chord could not be effective in unaccompanied singing. In fact Parry makes up for this in the orchestral accompaniment.

Ex. 37

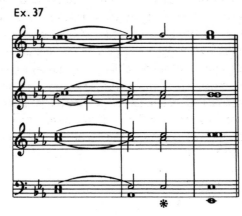

In the following, from Charles Wood's 'Hail, gladdening Light', we see a perfectly spaced chord at the resolution (2) of the added sixth chord*. It is the normal treatment of the sixth, which passes upwards to the third of the tonic chord.

Ex. 38

Now we come to a case in which the sixth of the chord is doubled. It occurs in E. W. Naylor's *Nunc Dimittis in A*.

Ex. 39

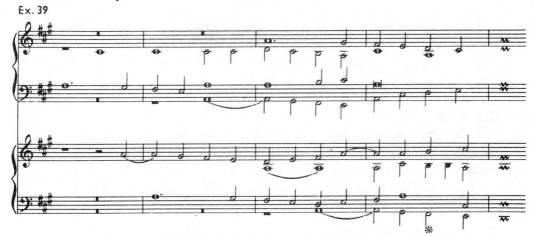

The sixth is the one which Kitson suggests should not be doubled. It is well to bear in mind that this note is discordant, rather than the fifth, which is the tonic of the key. The crux of the matter may be seen if the parts involving the sixth, B, are considered in their relation to the note A, the fifth of the chord, D, F sharp, A, B.

Clearly the B is taken in passing either from A to C sharp, or from C sharp to A. The note A is held in one voice while other voices pass either away from it or into it; in other words we see a second running into a unison *This is evidently an acceptable usage*, a fact which should be of interest to students, who are often in doubt about it. Theorists who forbid the movement of a second into a unison appear to forget how frequently this telescoping occurs in the sixteenth century and sometimes later, though from the eighteenth century onwards composers have run into the unison sparingly, ensuring that the discord of the second occurred on a weak metrical beat.

If we examine the first alto and the second alto in bar four, we note that in the former, C sharp moves direct to A, whereas in the latter it moves *through B to A*.

This seems somewhat difficult to reconcile with good writing. But if we bear in mind that A is mentally the concordant element, and that this clashing happens in the midst of a complex texture, there is nothing much to arrest the attention.

The following example, from Stanford's 'Ye Holy Angels bright', shows behaviour closely akin to the above in Ex. 39.

Ex. 40

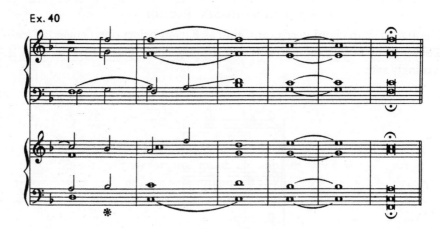

There is a running of a seventh into an eighth, and a sustaining of the tonic note as other parts move easily.

The same work provides the following example which is worth noting:

34

Ex. 41

The discordant note is C; it is not doubled, but twice we find C and B flat telescoping into D.

CONCLUSION

The added sixth chord may occur with the sixth note—the discordant element—occurring twice. Acceptable technique recognizes the running of a second into unison and a seventh into an eighth, the discord occurring upon the unstressed beat.

THE AUGMENTED SIXTH CHORDS

The Italian sixth chord needs care, and, as Kitson points out, demands a leap of a seventh by one of the parts. Its use in more than four parts, he adds, is exceedingly rare.

Ex. 42

The French sixth is shown by Kitson in the following treatment:

Ex. 43

If the first tenor fell to G, a better disposition of the second chord would result.

The German sixth, records Kitson, is nowadays, in four-part harmony, commonly resolved on to the dominant chord by indulgence in consecutive fifths, as follows:

Ex. 44

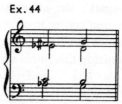

He shows the treatment in eight-part harmony as follows:

Ex. 44 (a)

It is interesting to find that in Mozart's time, these consecutive fifths (in four-part harmony) were not considered good at all. In a book on Thorough Bass thought to be founded on Mozart's practice, the following appears: 'When the augmented sixth is followed by a full common chord, or a suspended fourth with $\frac{8}{5}$, for instance $\frac{8}{5}_{43}$, it is not advisable to use the fifth, as consecutive fifths would ensue; unless the fifth is made to descend into the third'; for example:

Ex. 45

Example 45 is marked *good*, but the following is marked *bad*:

Ex. 45(a)

However Mozart may have regarded these consecutives in four-part harmony, there is no reason for us to alter our opinion today, as shown in Exx. 44 and 44*a*.

From days long before Mozart's the interpolation of another note of the harmony in between two main-beat consecutives was held to obliterate the effect of the consecutive,[1] a matter which our harmony textbooks appear to have overlooked. We see Stanford recognizing this in his work, as the following from 'Ye Holy Angels bright' shows.

Ex. 46

Note, too, Tenor I and Bass II moving *by leap*, from a second to a unison.

---

1. An intervening crotchet or quaver, short though its duration in the sixteenth century, frequently separates fifths (but not octaves) in Palestrina.

CHAPTER VI
Writing for Double-choir

KITSON gives some sound, if exacting, advice on writing for double-choir. He asserts that when the two four-part choirs are moving together, such features as consecutives by contrary motion and doubled leading-notes and discords should not occur in the same choir; also that the harmony given to each choir should be as far as possible complete in itself.

These suggestions should be followed by the student as broad principles. In no context should indulgences be shifts forced by poor technique. Nevertheless, it will be found that composers have broken Kitson's bounds. We have already seen that the leading-note occurs twice in the same choir and have concluded that this is legitimate technique (Chapter II, p. 16).

CONSECUTIVE FIFTHS BY CONTRARY MOTION IN THE SAME CHOIR

With regard to this, let us consult Stanford's 'Ye Holy Angels bright'.

Ex. 47

Here, clearly enough and strongly enough, the soprano and bass of the second choir proceed in consecutive fifths by contrary motion.

It can scarcely be conceived that there is anything objectionable or weak in this. The two choirs have joined forces; the effect is that of eight parts mingling together. In eight-part writing we have seen that this 'licence' (consecutive fifths in contrary motion) is acceptable technique (p. 20). In any case there is so much going on that any objectionable effect would be negligible, in fact obliterated. But what is obvious and most important is that the note F of the first soprano part is reinforced; and in this there is *purpose*, for it emphasizes the accent on the word *triumph*.

It is such considerations which give weight and authority to the licences or relaxations in which a composer may indulge. But the student should note that such procedure has nothing to do with weak technique.

CONSECUTIVE OCTAVES BY CONTRARY MOTION IN THE SAME CHOIR

Although there is rarely any need to use consecutive octaves by contrary motion in the *same* choir, yet, as has already been mentioned, *expressive purpose* is justification for such use.

Ex. 15 (p. 19) shows Tallis making use of consecutive octaves by contrary motion even in four-part work; but there was purpose behind his so doing (in this case, to make a free imitative entry).

Ex. 15a (p. 19) shows Bach using them in four-part harmony to give the best disposition of parts and flow of line.

Bach does not scruple even to use *occasional unisonal movement* in double-choir work, between voices of different choirs. His Motet 'Sing ye to the Lord' (Ex. 48) provides an instance of this. The unthoughtful observer might point to this as a slip on Bach's part. But is it? Bach was helping to make the fugal entry in the first tenor part more arresting.

Ex. 48

The following instance from Charles Wood's 'Hail, gladdening Light' shows consecutive octaves by contrary motion between the bass and soprano of the first choir, bar 5. It is worth careful examination.

Ex. 49

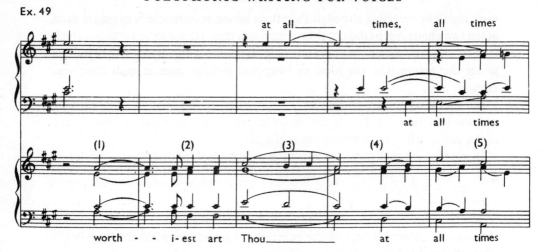

The composer could have avoided consecutives at this point. Why did he not do so? Because he judged it worth while, musically more effective, to give the first bass a similar entry to those of the first soprano and tenor immediately before, in bars 3 and 4. The effect is to increase the sense of purpose at this moment, to make us feel a greater urgency, as the bass enters at a shorter distance after the tenor, than the tenor did after the soprano. It would be difficult to find a purer writer of any period than Charles Wood; yet he clearly had no qualms about such an indulgence, because *expressive purpose went with it*. Further, it might be urged that even without any specific expressive purpose such as the above, the indulgence is justified as effecting the best disposition of harmony and parts, as in the instances by Bach and Vaughan Williams, Ex. 15*a* and 15*b*, p. 19. If purposeful disposition justifies such relaxations in four-part writing, how much more does it in writing for a greater number of parts.

In examination work, such procedure would be acceptable if used with good judgement, because examination problems are intended to test the ability to write in what might be termed the pure style as exemplified in the unaccompanied writing of acknowledged masters. *Artistic resource* is encouraged in preference to *pedestrian correctness*.

HARMONIC COMPLETENESS OF EACH CHOIR IN COMBINED SINGING

One author recommends that in double-choir work 'the harmony given to each choir should be as *far as possible* complete and satisfactory in itself'. This advice is well founded, but students are always bothered about the words 'as far as possible.'

It may be said that one of the finest examples of antiphonal and combined use of two choirs in the purest period is Palestrina's *Stabat Mater*. If we study this work it will be seen that although Palestrina aimed at complete harmony in each of the two choirs, yet he did not always maintain this. He did so 'as far as possible'. Our considerations may improve our judgement about this term, if they lead us to see the reason why the ideal of harmonic completeness in each choir was relaxed.

Harmonic completeness implies the presence of the *third* of a chord. Our purpose is to find out the conditions under which this note was omitted in one of the choirs when both were singing together.

It would seem that there are two cases which must be discussed separately:

A. When the third is not the leading-note.

B. When the third is the leading-note.

CASE A

Normally Palestrina follows the principle that each choir should contain the third of the chord; but there are many instances in which he did not carry this out.

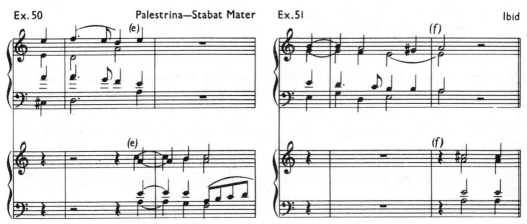

Ex. 50   Palestrina—Stabat Mater   Ex. 51   Ibid

In Ex. 50 (*e*) the first choir has no third on the last crotchet; the second choir entering on this beat has the third in one voice only, the alto.

In Ex. 51 (*f*) the first choir ends on a chord which has no third; the second choir, entering on the following crotchet beat, has the *major* third in the soprano.

The above examples show that when a choir is 'dropping out', it may dispense with the third of the chord, which note, however, is taken up by the second choir whose entry either overlaps, as at (*e*), or follows immediately, as at (*f*).

It is perhaps worth mentioning that at (*e*) the third might have been expected to be major, while at (*f*) it might have been expected to be minor (instead of the Tierce de Picardie as taken up in the second choir). The student should carefully consider such points for himself.

At (d) in Ex. 52 both choirs begin together. There seems no reason why the first choir should omit the third at the start, other than the fact that the alto part *creates movement* by proceeding from G to B (the third) against the static effect of the other parts.

At (*b*) above, it would seem that Palestrina omitted the third in the first choir —the retiring choir—on account of the activity around this note in the second choir. The effect is clearer, and the craftsmanship recognizes this.

At (*a*) above, the first choir omits the third, whereas the second choir doubles it. It is not quite the same as (*b*) just mentioned. This example is the kind of thing about which students are inquisitive. The omission seems to be due to the fact that the *line of some part* at that moment is of first importance and must not be interfered with. Thus after the antiphonal writing, and when the choirs are both engaged at (*a*), the soprano of the second choir holds the most important melodic line and rules the situation. If we endeavour to alter the parts and give complete harmony to each choir, we shall probably end by deciding that Palestrina's disposition of the harmony is best. Thus melodic line and placing of the parts seem to account for doubling the third in one choir and omitting it in the other.

In Ex. 54 the layout of the parts at (*c*) suggests that the omission of the third in the first choir is essential. The craftsmanship is improved by the omission and the imitative lines marked ⌐_⌐ ⌐_⌐ are the better for it. The student might try to alter the parts at this point.

Ex. 54

Ibid

Among twentieth-century writers of church music who have given us a number of compositions for double-choir, no one shows a purer style than Charles Wood. His respect for the *example* of Palestrina is seen in all his work. In his writing for two choirs there are instances of incomplete harmony in one of the choirs, similar to those of Palestrina; but he avoids this 'as far as possible', as does the Italian master. Bach also shows deference to the same principle, as a careful scrutiny of his 'Sing ye to the Lord' will testify.

CONCLUSION

Broadly speaking it may, therefore, be suggested that incompleteness in one of the choirs arises from the fact that musicianly judgement allows nothing to hinder good linear flow, clarity of texture, and harmonic balance (effective disposition of parts). Virtually, one might say that this treatment is the same as in eight-part vocal score and based upon the same musicianly judgement. Nevertheless, the ideal in double-choir composition is to maintain harmonic completeness in each choir.

CASE B

WHEN THE THIRD IS THE LEADING-NOTE

When the third is the leading-note it is noticeable that Palestrina, in his *Stabat Mater*, rarely uses it simultaneously in both choirs. Charles Wood's behaviour in this respect is often parallel to Palestrina's, though in instances it is freer. Let us examine the following examples:

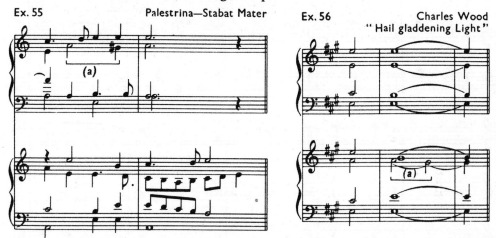

It will be seen that in both excerpts the leading-note occurs as a suspension ; its appearance is delayed and therefore it cannot occur in any other part for the moment. There are other similar instances in the *Stabat Mater*.

The following, from the same work by Palestrina, is interesting.

The leading-note, F sharp, is delayed by means of a suspension; when it appears in the alto part of the first choir, it also occurs in the tenor part of the second choir. This doubling is only momentary, for we see in the latter half of this bar that the leading-note is restricted to the alto of the first choir. A similar case occurs in the last two bars of the work. *It would seem that Palestrina's mind was to keep the leading-note for one voice only.*

Is there any reason for this? Consider for a moment the period in which Palestrina lived, when the Perfect Cadence, though common enough, possessed a character undimmed by association with *keys*. The bringing about of a perfect cadence necessitated, in certain of the ecclesiastical modes, the inflexion of the note below the final of the mode; thus in the Dorian Mode (final D) it was necessary to change the C to C sharp. This was termed 'musica ficta'; often there was no written indication of this inflexion, as it was understood by the singers who practised together and sang the service music day by day. The effect of this cadence, in modal surroundings, was colourful; so much so, that the C sharp, the altered note, was not to be strengthened by appearing more than once, even in double-choir work. Very often its appearance was delayed by suspension.

Another very important point was that this new note, C sharp, had *inevitably to rise* to the final of the mode, D. *It was its function to do so.* Thus we see how it came to be called the leading-note: it always led up to the Final (or Tonic as we now call it), for it occurred only at the cadence.

These are the reasons, it may be said, why Palestrina shows such care about the leading-note in his double-choir and eight-part writing. *It was the colour-giving sound, and its natural function was to rise to the Tonic.*

But in non-modal music the Perfect Cadence was the *normal* occurrence, the ordinary effect. No longer was there anything novel or striking about it. The colour-creating power of the leading-note was not so strong. Bach realized this and, as we have seen, did not refrain from using it in more than one voice in six- as well as eight-part writing. He also used it simultaneously in both choirs in double-choir composition. In these cases one of the leading-notes usually fulfilled its original function and rose to the Tonic, thereby defining the more important melodic line; the other usually fell, but not always.

It may be noticed even in Bach's four-part chorales that the leading-note is quite freely treated. Although normally it does not fall when used in the melody, yet Bach allows it to do so when he feels the melody calls for it (see Ex. 61). In an inner part, at the Perfect Cadence, it *falls* as often as not to the fifth of the Tonic Chord which follows: obviously, for the purpose of giving fullness to the final harmony. We shall see in Ex. 62 with what freedom Tallis treated the leading-note, even 150 years before Bach's day.

This loss in colour-strength of the leading-note, as the major and minor scale system superseded the several ecclesiatical modes, explains, it may be said, the freer use of it by composers as time went on. The tendency to regard the leading-note as merely the third of the dominant chord, and to treat it as a free note, grew. This attitude towards the seventh degree of the scale is very obvious in

Handel, who ignores any restriction whatsoever on its use: we find it employed with complete freedom in the chief melodic part, even in four-part writing. His oratorio *Judas Maccabeus* provides instances of this; see the following Exx. 58 and 59, where the leading-note falls by leap to a note of the next chord which is new harmony.

Ex. 58 (Chorus—"Mourn ye afflicted children")

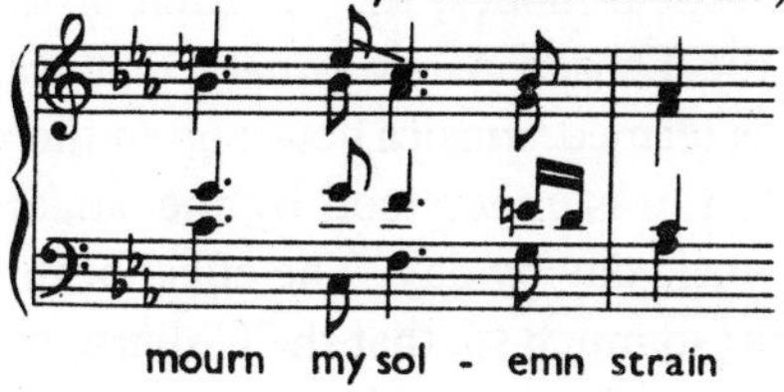

Ex. 59 (Chorus No. 27)

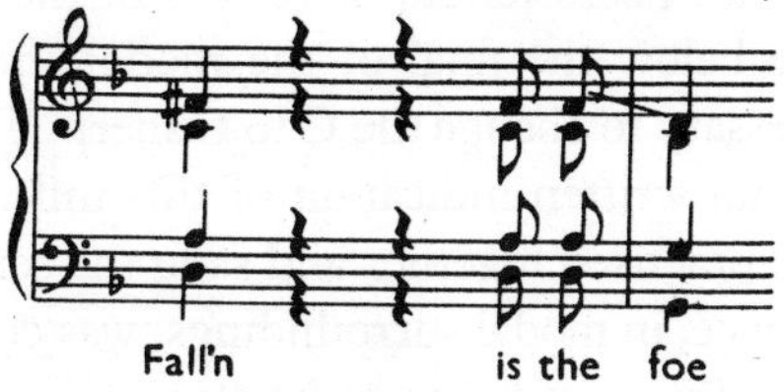

Surely it is high time that the nonsense about 'the leading-note must rise' was replaced by teaching which is in line with the *practice* of great composers. Instruction which ignores such practice is sterile.

Instances similar to the above occur in the melodies of hymns and chorales. Let the following suffice:

Ex. 60 "Heathlands" H. Smart (1813-73)

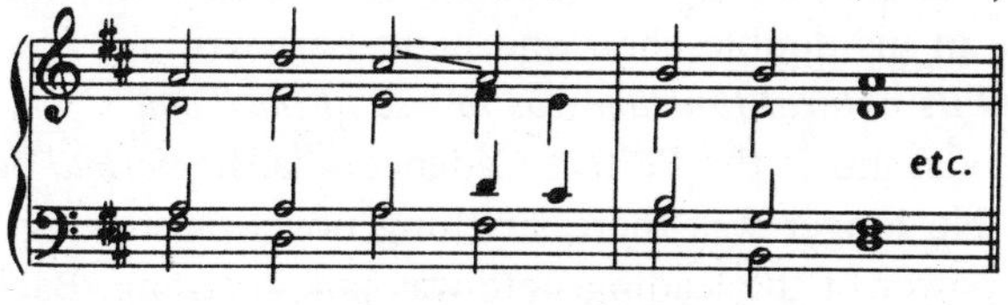

Ex. 61 Bach (from Christmas Oratorio)

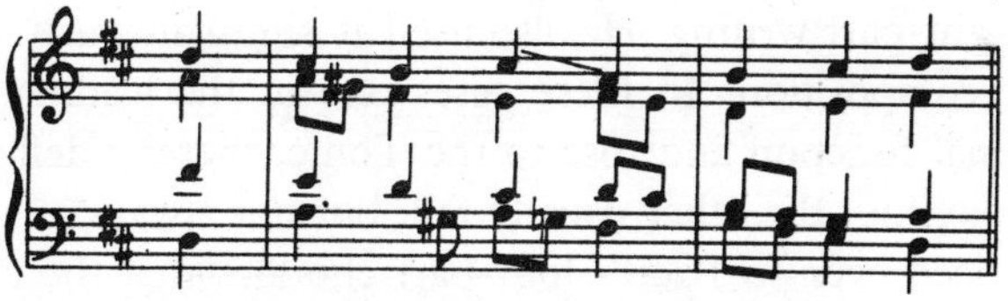

Scrutinize Tallis's Ordinal (9th tune). It shows clearly enough the leading-note falling by leap to create better vocal parts for the alto and tenor singers. This reveals the mind of one of our great English composers, who evidently allowed nothing to stand in the way of *musical* writing.

Ex. 62

Tallis Ordinal (9th tune)

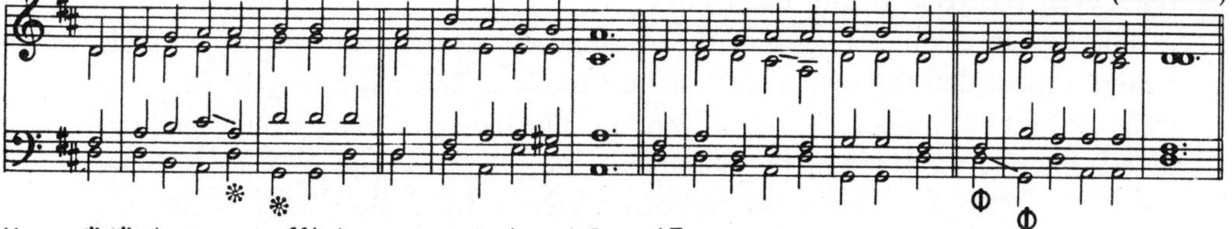

Note at ❊ ❊ the consecutive fifths in contrary motion between Bass and Tenor

Note at Φ Φ the consecutive octaves in contrary motion between Bass and Treble

It was said on p. 45 (Exx. 55 and 56) that Charles Wood's writing was parallel with Palestrina's in certain instances—involving the third as leading-note—and in others much freer. We see this in such examples as the following:

Ex. 63

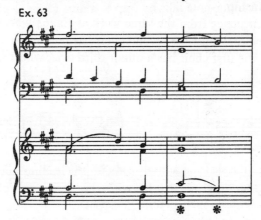

In the above from 'Hail, gladdening Light' there are points other than those concerning the leading-note, which are worth the student's consideration. The leading-note is doubled in the same choir here. In the following we see the leading-note in *both* choirs:

Charles Wood, *Magnificat and Nunc Dimittis* (Collegium Regale).

Ex. 64

This ends the consideration of Case B.

Students often ask if it is necessary to maintain harmonic completeness in each choir, when two choirs are singing together. They say: 'Is not this virtually eight-part writing?' On p. 21 it was stated that this is so, but that in sixteenth-century work, and in later work in this pure style, it is well to follow Palestrina's ideals 'as far as possible'.

Nevertheless, relaxations do frequently occur in more modern work, as we have seen. It is, however, safe to say that they are not due to any weakness in technical skill, but, on the contrary, are the outcome of careful thought combined with sure craftsmanship.

Here is such an instance from the same work as Ex. 64 where the first choir has a major third twice, whilst the second choir has no third at all (at ★). In the following bar at ⊕ the first choir has a minor third twice whilst the second choir has no third.

Ex. 65

This chapter brings to a close the broad considerations of what may be termed straightforward technique in regard to six- and eight-part writing. It is hoped that the points mentioned may have given the student a clearer view of the whole matter, and that he may be more confident in tackling his own work. He should not be content with correctness; because, although this is proof of some ability to handle a number of parts, yet it may lack the true essentials of good work which are musical quality and grace.

Examination questions are set in order to prove that the student possesses a well-founded technique and a sense of style. A problem in the sixteenth-century style should observe the characteristics of that period; it should not be a hotch-potch.

The following chapters are concerned with post-sixteenth-century writing and free composition, and also matters relating to the expansion of vocal technique and expression.

CHAPTER VII

Direct and Slightly Delayed Consecutive Octaves and Fifths

WE cannot examine a number of works ranging over a long period, written for voices in many parts, without discovering instances of direct consecutive octaves and fifths which compel our attention and inquiry. Further, we shall see that these works also show the presence of slightly delayed (i.e. *close*) consecutive octaves and fifths which arouse our curiosity; in fact, so frequent are such instances that their scrutiny is forced upon us: they cannot be passed over without comment.

The student may hope to find consecutive octaves and fifths treated separately; but it has in fact been found impossible to keep them in compartments that do not overlap, and it is hoped that he will find no difficulty as he reads the chapter.

DIRECT AND SLIGHTLY DELAYED CONSECUTIVE OCTAVES

By slightly delayed consecutives I mean such as the following:

Ex. 66 Palestrina : Missa Æterna Christi Munera "

Ex. 67

Ex. 68 Palestrina-Motet " Paucitus dierum "

Ex. 69

J. S. Bach—Chorale.

Ex. 70   Battishill (1738-1801)—"Amidst the myrtles "

A summary of the position as regards prohibited consecutive octaves is given by R. O. Morris in his book, *Foundations of Practical Harmony*. He writes as follows:

'Consecutive octaves are forbidden because they are manifestly not true part-writing. One voice that echoes another at an octave distance is not an independent voice part at all. That is because the interval of the octave is so perfect a consonance that the separate identity of the two voices is lost. Even a trained ear, momentarily off its guard, might easily mistake an octave for a single note. . . . Precisely the same is true of the fifth. . . . That is, briefly, why classical tradition forbids the use of consecutive fifths and octaves in real part-writing (doubling a bass or melody at the octave for purposes of timbre and resonance is, of course, quite another matter).'

This statement is readily appreciated, but one is reminded of those early times when boys' voices were first brought into choirs because of the bright effect they created when singing in octaves with the men. This, it would appear, emphasizes the fact that parts moving in octaves give prominence, and draw attention to melodic outline. Thus, quite beside the fact that one voice echoing another at an octave distance is not an independent voice part at all, it is clear that the objection to parts moving together in octaves has for its reason that prominence is given to a particular line of tone; furthermore, such prominence causes an unbalance in effect (in relation to the remaining parts).

Such direct consecutive octaves, continuous or even occasional, appear to have been condemned outright by textbook writers, one after the other. In writing for voices in few parts—such as four—this ruling has been generally observed since the major and minor scale system was established. (But even Bach occasionally allowed a pair of octaves or fifths to remain.)

As to what might be acceptable in writing for more than four or five voices, little that is definite about relaxations has been mentioned by theorists.

Nevertheless, the frequency with which pairs of consecutive octaves, fifths, and even unisons occur in the six- and eight-part writing of great composers can leave no doubt in our minds as to their legitimacy. The masters did not frown upon them. They evidently considered the effect of consecutives to be so unobtrusive that there was no necessity to rule them out from technical resource.

Morris adds:

'So far as it goes, this prohibition (of consecutives) is granted on reason and psychological truth. What is absurd about the tradition is that it ignores the effect of added parts, of position, and of new elements in the chord (discords). It is not possible to say that the two fifths $\frac{d-e}{g-a}$ are equally apparent in all the following:

Ex. 71

'At (b) the effect is less noticeable than at (a); at (c) and (d) it is not noticeable at all. Compare the following:

Ex. 72

'At (a) the fifths between the outer parts arrest the ear at once; at (b) they do not, for the attention is distracted and held by the dissonant elements in the chords; unless one took the trouble to reflect on and analyse what one had just heard one would never notice the fifths at all.

'Text-book tradition, always blind to psychological realities would blue-pencil all of these impartially, and the student sitting in the examination room has to bear that in mind.'

The above quotations and comments, with which one agrees, point to the fact that such consecutives become most noticeable when exposed between the extreme parts. When they happen between inner parts, not necessarily adjacent, they are *enclosed*, as it were, hidden, or covered. Obviously, therefore, the more parts there are to enclose them, the less will the ear detect them, quite apart from whether we think they are objectionable or not; consequently such a view should enter into the matter of relaxations in writing for many parts. Even in four parts the effect of consecutive fifths between the *extreme* parts is obliterated by dissonant elements, as is pointed out by Morris; so much the more should such an observation be borne in mind when five or more voices are being combined.

We have seen in Exx. 15, 15*a*, 15 *b* (all of them in four parts) two voices starting from the unison and proceeding by contrary movement to an octave. The examples are from Tallis, Bach, Vaughan Williams, musicians living in widely different periods. We learned something from these examples, and saw composers using good musical common sense, though their ways do not coincide with textbook instructions. Even though we may consider that octaves by contrary motion are not as noticeable as direct octaves, nevertheless the theorists have never given them their blessing. But the following from Tallis's *Magnificat in Mode Seven with verses in Fauxbourdon* apparently flouts all theorists' rules, for we see direct octaves in a five-part score.

Ex. 73

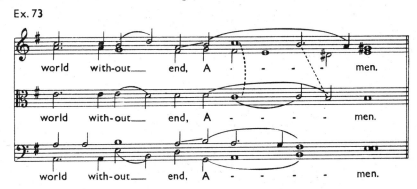

As to whether Tallis considered it an unpardonable piece of behaviour that the soprano echoes the tenor at an octave's distance and is not an independent voice part at all, I do not know. Tallis wrote contrapuntally because he thought linearly, and I feel convinced that he was fully aware of what he was doing in the above example. Neither his eyes nor his ears (*far more important*) were closed.

As for the delayed octaves between soprano and alto, they were a means of creating a little expressive piquancy; a simple enough means, indeed, but deliciously effective. We seem to have forgotten or at least neglected such a procedure; but, sad to say, it is only one of the many points of technique which have been lost through the forbidding voice of theorists, in the interests of what they imagine to be pure style. Their ideas of purity beget insipidity. Eric Gill said something to the effect that in both art and life the refining process can be carried on until there is nothing much left. A South African poet, Roy Campbell, expresses the same sentiments forthrightly and wittily in his quatrain *On Some South African Novelists.*

> You praise the firm restraint with which they write—
> I'm with you there, of course:
> They use the snaffle and the curb all right,
> But where's the bloody horse?

Let us return to Ex. 73. Can we account for Tallis's direct octaves? The answer, it may be ventured, is *yes*: but first, let attention be drawn to a number of other instances of consecutive and slightly delayed consecutive octaves in vocal scores of many parts:

Ex. 74 Pearsall "Great God of Love"

The unisons at *a–a* were surely not an oversight on Pearsall's part. As we have already seen in Ex. 31, p. 29, and as we shall see again, this is one of the relaxations indulged in and recognized by great composers in their writing for many voice parts. Evidently they did not consider that such 'lapses from grace' had any significance, nor that they were easily detectable.

An interesting point emerges from these examples just mentioned and from Ex. 48, p. 39, by Bach. Consecutive octaves, unisons, and fifths may be justified on two opposite counts. They may be so bound up in the texture or so short-lived as to be detectable only with difficulty, and therefore neglible in effect; on the other hand, they may be used deliberately to draw attention to a melodic curve or a point of emphasis. The Ex. 48 by Bach illustrates this latter effect; while Ex. 31 by Naylor, and Ex. 74 by Pearsall illustrate the former.

With further reference to Ex. 74, we see at *b–b* slightly delayed consecutive octaves, as the tenor part has rests. *Must we concede that the rests obliterate the effect of consecutiveness? The answer is 'Yes'*, as further evidence to follow decidedly proves.

At *c–c* in this Ex. 74 is another instance of what are virtually direct consecutive octaves, or, if you will, a seventh telescoping into an octave (as already seen in Exx. 40 and 41, pp. 34 and 35).

In the Ex. 75 below, also by Pearsall and from the same work as Ex. 74, we see unisons at *a–a*. The parts are hidden and absorbed by the surrounding texture. The first soprano and second tenor *b–b* should be observed; they are merely a type of delayed consecutives.

Ex. 75

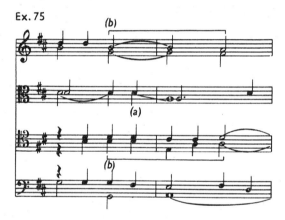

The following is taken from E. W. Naylor's *Magnificat and Nunc Dimitis in A*

Ex. 76

The theme is in the soprano of the second choir with the tenor running in parallel sixths. The second choir tenor is *shadowed*, as it were, by the first choir tenor.

From the same work the following excerpt is taken:

Ex. 77

The theme is in the soprano of the second choir; the tenor of the first choir at *a–a* may be regarded as emphasizing it at that high point *E*. At *b–b* the effect is again one of *shadowing* the theme; but in this somewhat loaded texture the consecutives are absorbed. The result is that of strengthening the main notes of the thematic outline, as in orchestration.

Let us examine two passages from Stanford's 'Ye Holy Angels bright'.

Ex. 78 Allegro

At *a–a* there are direct consecutive octaves. Stanford could have avoided them; they are very short-lived. The first chord in the second bar is best distributed as it stands.

Ex. 79 Ibid

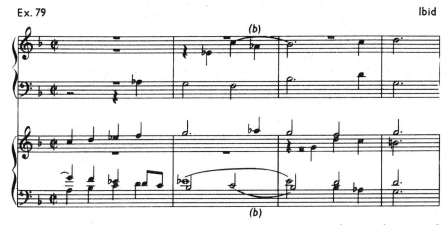

At *b–b* are consecutive octaves on two successive main beats: they are *close* consecutives of the Palestrinian type, and merely strengthen the 'tag' in the alto of the first choir—a kind of *shadowing*.

Let us examine Schütz's 'Sing unto the Lord'.

Ex. 80

We note at *c–c*, *d–d close* consecutive fifths; very common occurrences.

At *a–a*, *b–b* are direct consecutive octaves *with a rest intervening* in each case. These instances provide more evidence supporting the answer 'Yes' to the question 'Must we concede that rests obliterate the effect of consecutiveness?' (see p. 55). It is a matter which has bearing upon the Tallis Magnificat (Ex. 73, p. 53) where there are direct octaves *without* intervening rests.

Let it suffice at the moment to draw attention (in Ex. 80) to a point which will be further discussed later on, that on the word 'eternity' a thought has been completely expressed. After it, the *Amen* adds, by its meaning, a corroboration of the thought or thoughts just concluded. There is a separation of the verbal ideas, emphasized by the crotchet rest preceding the word *Amen*. The mind no longer feels the continuity of an unbroken phrase, and is not arrested by the slightly delayed consecutive octaves. This, as stated already, leads to the conclusion that *the use of a rest in this way must be accepted as a legitimate device in the technique of writing in many parts*; its similar use in many other instances (some of which will be quoted) adds weight to this decision.

The following, from the same work as Ex. 80 by Schütz, shows that he evidently had no objection to *close* consecutive octaves or fifths, such as are seen at *a–a*, *b–b*.

Ex. 81

Neither had Parry, as the following excerpt from his *Blest Pair of Sirens* proves:

Ex. 82

Orchestra

At *a–a* are consecutive unisons delayed by a rest, which gives the first alto the opportunity of the suspension.

At *b–b* we see *close* consecutive octaves; I regard them as such despite the effect of the A natural on the fourth crotchet (a very weak part of the bar). They are the kind which students fight shy of.

The minds of Schütz and Parry clearly agree on these points, although they lived at periods separated by more than two centuries.

The next example is from Gordon Jacob's 'To Music to becalm his fever'. In this fine work for eight-part unaccompanied choir, the student will find an example of vocal polyphony by a modern writer that will amply repay his attention.

The direct consecutive octaves and fifths at *a–a*, *b–b* are obviously of the kind that do not arrest the ear, enclosed as they are in this texture. The consecutive fifths at *c–c* are certainly intentional, since they could easily have been avoided. The flow of the first bass part is improved; furthermore, the second tenor crosses their path and so makes their detection less easy. They may be regarded also

59

Ex 83

as possessing the binding and enriching attributes of occasional consecutive fifths, as mentioned on pp. 10–11; in fact they create a natural sonority.

Although many more instances of direct and close consecutive octaves could be placed before the student, those already provided amply suffice to illustrate acceptable relaxation in the technique of writing in many parts.

Let attention now be turned to the consideration of *direct and slightly delayed consecutive fifths*.

The following is quoted from *The English Madrigal Composers*, by E. H. Fellowes, written in 1916:

'Throughout the whole history of modern music, as dating from 1600, the use of such progression [consecutive fifths] has been regarded in academic circles as an error of the first class, standing on the same level as a false quantity in Latin verse.

There is no doubt as to the educational value for students of a training which enforces the strictest observation of definite and reasonable rules of grammar, nor is there any doubt that all the greatest music of the Classical Period was composed with a universal recognition of the rule that consecutive fifths and octaves were to be absolutely excluded; and it is a fact that scarcely any instance of such progressions can be quoted from the whole of the works of such composers as Bach, Mozart, Haydn, Schubert, Beethoven and Brahms. Not only so, but kindred rules dealing with "hidden fifths" and other such matters, grew to be respected with almost equal strictness. But in modern days composers are throwing such rules to the winds, and it cannot be denied that objection to these forbidden progressions is often based on no more than academic affectation, and not purely on aesthetic grounds. It is sometimes forgotten that the rule about fifths was being deliberately disregarded by several prominent musicians in Italy as well as in England at the close of the sixteenth century; and the fact that the world's greatest musicians in the period roughly lying between 1560 and 1900 observed it strictly does not necessarily establish it for all time. It is sometimes forgotten, also, that the earliest kind of harmonized music took the form of singing a piece of music right through in consecutive fifths.

In connexion with this subject the practice of the English madrigalists is full of interest. Direct pairs of fifths seldom occur in the writings of the majority of these composers, and practically never in those of Byrd, Morley, Wilbye, and Weelkes; but such a composer as Farnaby seems to have felt no great objection to them, and the large number of such progressions in his Canzonets cannot possibly be explained on the grounds of negligence or incompetence. It is clear that he deliberately disregarded the rule.

But as regards "hidden fifths", and pairs of consecutive fifths or octaves on strong beats, the madrigalists appear to have felt no sort of restriction; for throughout the madrigal-literature there are numberless instances of such progressions as:

It cannot for a moment be pretended that these details amount to blemishes, or that they detract one iota from the artistic value of music as a whole.'

The above examples provided by Dr. Fellowes show that what are called *close* consecutives used to be common practice among a fine body of English madrigal composers. Similar examples have already been given from composers other than those of the English School, but now quotations are given from the three-part Mass of William Byrd, one of the greatest among the musicians of all nations.

Ex. 84

Were the rest omitted at (*a*) in the uppermost part, there would be direct consecutive fifths with the bass. It may therefore be assumed that in Byrd's estimation *the rest obliterated any such effect*. Surely this is further confirmation of the decision already set down that the use of a rest in this way must be accepted as legitimate technique. That great composers regarded it as such is beyond doubt, but it is a point that has been forgotten—or wellnigh forgotten —in our teaching for a long time. Dr. Fellowes observed that although the rule about direct consecutive fifths was adhered to in the period lying roughly between 1560 and 1900, it is not necessarily established for all time. This is indeed true: reference to numberless works composed during this period will confirm the statement. Giles Farnaby snapped his fingers at the rule, and so did others in England and elsewhere during the seventeenth century and the Classical Period.

In the eighteenth century, Maurice Greene (d. 1755) indulged in the following, which is taken from his anthem 'Lord, let me know mine end'.

Ex. 85

The effect of these direct fifths must have satisfied Greene, and evidently that was all that mattered to him. Greene was not one of the *great* composers, but his work commands our respect; the same may be said of Battishill (1738–1801) who, as far as breaking rules is concerned, seems to be akin to Farnaby. Here is a couple of bars from a five-part secular work by him, which shows, as does Greene's example, that our composers went about things in their own way.

Ex. 86   " Amidst the myrtles "

Of course these consecutives were not marked in the actual written music; they were left for everyone to see (and think what they liked). Not so, however, in

1920, when Charles Macpherson, the organist of St. Paul's Cathedral, published his *Communion Service in E flat*. In order to inform all and sundry that a pair of consecutive fifths occur—and that he *knew* they were there—he caused them to be marked as follows:

Ex. 87

Is it too much to suggest that Macpherson's frankness spared him the bother of answering many letters?

Consider now our composers of the latter half of the seventeenth century.

Dr. W. G. Whittaker in his *Collected Essays* makes observations on Purcell's harmony. He writes:

'Consecutives are like blackberries in autumn. That he recked nothing of "fifths" is shown in Exx. 29 and 30; Ex. 31 barely escapes them by the skin of its teeth, while Ex. 32 gives us, quite nakedly, an augmented followed by a perfect. Lock (Exx. 33 and 34) is no less casual about them; indeed in the second he shamelessly combines consecutive fifths with consecutive sevenths! It is evident that the practice of the next two centuries (18th and 19th), when such parallel movement was looked upon as dangerous licence, was not *yet* a matter of harmonic belief.'

By *yet* in the concluding sentence, Whittaker referred to the time of Purcell.

Here are the examples referred to above, according to Whittaker's numbering:

Lock's shamelessly combining consecutive fifths and sevenths strengthens Dr. Morris's statement that 'what is absurd about the tradition (the prohibition of consecutives) is that it ignores the effect of added parts, of position, and of new elements in the chord (discords)'. There can be no doubt that the effect of consecutive fifths is reduced in its power to arrest the ear by the presence of such discordance as the seventh.

It is certain that *before* 1560, direct consecutive octaves and fifths were commonly used, at any rate in five-part writing, and proof of this could be given by quotations from Robert Fayrfax (d. 1521) and John Redford (d. 1543). Robert Whyte (d. 1574) has consecutive fifths, separated by rests (like other instances which have already been seen), in his Motet 'Miserere mei, Deus'.

Ex. 88

As to close or slightly delayed consecutives, such as we have seen by Byrd, Palestrina, and others, they abound in the scores of these early sixteenth-century composers, particularly five-part scores.

All these examples prove that Fellowes is right when, after reviewing the methods and idioms of the English Madrigalists, he says:

'Enough has been said to show that rules of Counterpoint as understood by the English Madrigalists are by no means in complete agreement with the ordinary modern text-books. These text-books, many of which have great merits of their own and serve the all-important purpose of enforcing a severe discipline upon students, *deal with Counterpoint as it was understood by the musicians and theorists of the Continent*, rather than the Counterpoint which the great English polyphonic composers wrote, either in their Church music or Madrigals.'[1]

This statement is assuredly supported by the following account of a controversy about consecutive fifths separated by short rests occurring in Corelli (Sonata Third, Opera 2da). It is recorded in Burney, *A General History of Music* (London,

---

[1] Continuing, Fellowes states: that 'English music-students have never been given the chance of receiving a training based upon their national traditions'. No one can deny this; there is, however, reason to believe that this serious matter is receiving earnest attention today.

1789). I refer to the edition published by G. T. Foulis & Co., London, 1935, volume 2, pp. 537 and 538.

'Colonna (*c.* 1637–95) had a controversy with Corelli in 1685, concerning the consecution of fifths in the first movement of the third sonata of his opera 2da. Every lover of music will be sorry that the charge against Corelli should be well-founded; but it must be owned that the base is indefensible in the passage which has been condemned by Colonna, and was not likely to have passed uncensored even in an age more licentious than that of Corelli.

Antimo Liberati, with whom Colonna was in correspondence at the time of this controversy, seems to defend Corelli's violation of the known rule against the consecution of fifths, in a letter written in 1685, *Sopra un sequito di quinte*, in which he reasons thus:

"If a quaver rest, or even a semiquaver, were not sufficient to satisfy the rule against fifths and eights, a composer writing in many parts would have very narrow limits for the expansion of his genius and fancy, or for varying the harmony." But [continues Burney], with due respect for the authority of Antimo Liberati, and with peace to the ashes of the gentle Corelli, the passage is unwarrantable, and seems the more inexcusable, as several better basses were easy to find, without altering the design, or destroying the effect of the trebles.'

Here is the passage referred to and the *better basses* supplied by Burney.

Ex. 89   Fragment of Corelli, Sonata Third, Opera 2da.

As to whether Burney's suggested *better* basses improve upon Corelli's or not, the reader will decide for himself. Do they not reveal the type of narrow-mindedness which characterizes the theorist and divorces his judgement from that of the artist, the *creative* musician?

It should be noted that Liberati mentions that *even a semiquaver* is sufficient to satisfy the rule against consecutive fifths and eighths. With him I entirely agree, and venture to pursue this further with relation to the Tallis example, No. 73, p.53, in which occur *direct* consecutive octaves.

So far consecutives have been seen, separated by a *crotchet* rest even in three-part work by Byrd, and up to eight-part by Schütz, Pearsall, Parry, and others; but not by a rest *smaller* than a crotchet.

Is not the separation of one musical idea or thought from another, coinciding with the completion of sense in the text, a similar rest—a *short* space of silence? I suggest that this is sufficient reason to justify such consecutives as occur in Ex. 73 by Tallis.

The 'Gloria Patri' finishes with the word *end*. The next word *Amen* is separated from it. Thus, with the word *end*, Tallis completes the sense of the words and the musical idea together. From that point our minds go forward to the restart of the music with the word *Amen*. This restart destroys any continuity of the sort that would be felt in the midst of a passage or phrase. That is the point which must be appreciated. Therefore there is no feeling of consecution between the parts that move in octaves (first soprano and alto). Although a semiquaver rest is not *written*, it is *felt*, and *made* in *taking breath*. If anyone doubts this, let him consider a similar and very familiar instance. Who feels any effect of consecutives between the last chord of a verse in a hymn and the first chord of the next verse? Or between two verses of a Psalm? Both are instances merely of the separation of one thought from another. In the singing of Psalms the music is wellnigh continuous from verse to verse, particularly when the performance is antiphonal.[1]

Such reasoning as the above no doubt never entered Tallis's mind at all; but the idea that he made an error—an odd one here and there—should be banished from our thought. Moreover, we have here an aspect of technique by no means negligible, at which the finger of scornful superiority should no longer be pointed. Such procedure as Tallis shows should not be brushed aside as though belonging to a bygone age less enlightened than ours, and therefore to be discarded. Men of his calibre were indeed quite as wise as any who are concerned with the making of music today. Surely if our study of past masters means anything at all, it should lead us to *discover* their art and craft, and see to it that none of it is lost in our own.

Another matter which has bearing upon the effect of consecutives is tempo. A short-lived consecution counts for little, as evidently Purcell and Stanford considered (Exs. 29 and 30, p. 28, and Ex. 78, p. 56).

Further, as Whittaker remarks, 'in Purcell's day'—and may I add, later too— 'parallel movement was not a matter of harmonic belief'. This, no doubt, is a

---

[1] Other quotations similar to the one by Tallis could be taken from the works of other composers of that period, which show that this attitude was not singular to Tallis, or that he had overlooked a slip.

true and far-reaching statement. Composers were concerned with melodic lines more than with harmonic rules; after all, the major and minor key-system (as we know it) had not set in, and musicians' methods of working, their attitude of mind and ear, were not encumbered with the regulations associated with that system. In any case, such men as Greene and Battishill, who lived in the eighteenth century in the midst of that system, preferred not to allow its harmonic impositions to interfere with, or override, the freedom of melodic thought and curve. This truth, simple as it may seem, has deep roots; it is, too, the spirit which has never died out among English composers and which in our own day is more alive than it has been for a long time.

CONCLUSIONS

Direct consecutive octaves and fifths have been used in scores of five or more parts (and even of fewer) and are justified on the following main grounds:

1. Their insignificant effect on the mind when they are enclosed or absorbed by the texture, and when their path is crossed by other voices;
2. Their effect being diluted or overshadowed by the presence of a rest or rests;
3. Their effect being nullified by the act of breathing (equivalent to a short rest), which separates one idea from another;
4. Their effect being mitigated by the presence of discordant element or elements;
5. Their effect being negligible when short-lived;
6. Their harmonic effect being considered subordinate to the freedom and power of melodic flow and curve;
7. Their binding and enriching power, creating a natural sonority;
8. Their effect for its own sake and purpose.

Slightly delayed octaves and fifths in great variety have been common practice in all periods.

NOTE

Questions set in sixteenth-century style should be treated with the proper technique.

Questions set in later styles and in free composition invite the technique discussed in Chapters I–VII; but it should be used in convincing manner, with discretion and good judgement (see also p. 113, A and B).

SUMMARY OF CONCLUSIONS

(CHAPTERS I–VII)

The Case of the Leading-note (CHAP. II)

  i. In six-part writing

    The leading-note may be doubled, but not indiscriminately; melodic line, harmonic balance in the disposition of the parts must always control the situation.

  ii. In eight-part and double-choir writing

    The leading note may be doubled, and possibly trebled (Bach); and there is no restriction even though the leading note is in the bass. As in the case of six-part writing such treatment should not be indiscriminate.

Consecutive Octaves and Fifths by Contrary Motion (CHAP. III)

  i. In six-part writing

    Indulgence in consecutive octaves and fifths in contrary motion has been common practice.

  ii. In eight-part score

    Consecutive octaves and fifths by contrary motion have been recognized as acceptable technique. Consecutive octaves by contrary motion in the two bass parts need not be restricted to two moves.

  iii. In double-choir writing

    Consecutive octaves and fifths by contrary motion have been a general practice. There is no restriction upon the number of moves of such consecutive octaves occurring between the two bass parts.

The Dominant Seventh Chord (CHAP. IV)

  i. The seventh may be doubled and given the twofold resolution usually associated with the chord in the second inversion, even though the chord is in root position or any inversion.

  ii. The seventh may be doubled and one of them treated irregularly; that is, not by step. It may leap to a note of the next chord towards which there is magnetic pull, or to a note readily felt by the singer.

Secondary Seventh Chords (CHAP. IV)

The seventh may be doubled. The treatment is usually one of the following:

  i. Both may remain to be a part of the next chord.

  ii. One may remain, and the other leap.

  iii. One may rise by step, and the other fall by step.

  iv. One may fall by step, and the other fall by leap.

  v. One may rise by leap, and the other fall by leap.

  vi. One may remain as a suspension, and the other leap.

  vii. Both may leap.

The influence of magnetic pull should be borne in mind.

The Added Sixth Chord (CHAP. V)

The added sixth chord may occur with the sixth (the discordant element) occurring twice. Acceptable technique recognizes the running of a second into a unison, and a seventh into an eighth.

Writing for Double-choir (CHAP. VI)

i. Consecutive fifths *by contrary motion* may occur in the same choir when the two choirs are singing together—good purpose should be served in so doing; it should not result from weak technique.

ii. Consecutive octaves *by contrary motion* may occur in the same choir when the two choirs are singing together—some good purpose should be served by their occurrence. It should be an artistic resource in any case.

iii. Occasional unisons used with definite expressive purpose may be indulged in (Bach, Ex. 43).

iv. Harmonic *completeness of each choir* in combined singing is the ideal, but even Palestrina did not always achieve it (see pp. 40 et seq.). Generally, the importance of melodic line and the placing of the parts to give the most satisfying effect account for doubling the third in one choir and omitting it in the other.

v. *When the major third is the leading-note* Palestrina rarely uses it simultaneously in both choirs; his mind was evidently to reserve it for one part only.

vi. In non-modal music the leading-note may be doubled and may appear twice in the same choir in combined singing.

vii. In non-modal music there are no restrictions upon the movement of the leading-note. Although frequently it rises to the tonic as was its function in the work of Palestrina and his contemporaries, yet there is no necessity for it to do so.

Direct and Slightly Delayed Consecutive Octaves and Fifths (CHAP. VII)

Direct consecutive octaves and fifths have been used in vocal scores of five or more parts and are justified on the following main grounds:

i. Their insignificant effect on the mind when they are enclosed or absorbed by the texture, and when their path is crossed by another voice or voices;

ii. Their effect being diluted or overshadowed by the presence of a rest or rests;

iii. Their effect being nullified by the act of breathing (equivalent to a short rest), which separates one idea from another;

iv. Their effect being mitigated by the presence of one or more discordant elements;

v. Their effect being negligible when short-lived;

vi. Their harmonic effect being considered subordinate to the freedom and power of melodic flow and curve;

vii. Their binding and enriching power, creating a natural sonority;

viii. Their effect for its own sake and purpose.

Slightly delayed consecutives in great variety have been common practice in all periods.

CHAPTER VIII

Further Exploration of Technique

COMPOSERS, as every musician knows, are their own masters; that is, they can write as they like, ignore every textbook rule under the sun, and extend relaxations to any length according to the promptings of their imagination. They know, or *should* know, if their choral writing is *really* suitable for voices or not; and they should realize that voices are not orchestral instruments from which any intervals are forthcoming so long as fingers are directed to the appropriate places. Of course, music for unaccompanied voices could not remain as Palestrina and Byrd bequeathed it to us; technical progress, though not obvious at certain periods, nevertheless is continuous. The highly trained choir of today has far outstripped the technique of choralism even of the year 1900.

Nevertheless, pure choral music is not the same medium as instrumental music, in which sphere modern harmonic progress has mostly, though not exclusively, developed. To produce a note of a certain pitch by voice, the singer must first *feel* it; otherwise he cannot *take* it. This is the crux of the matter concerning the expansion of vocal technique and expression.[1] Too much stress cannot be laid upon it, as will be demonstrated in the following pages.

Modern choral music demands greater efforts of *concentration* on the part of the singer; this is obvious when we think of, say, Haydn's *Creation*, Mendelssohn's *Elijah*, Dvořák's *Stabat Mater*, on the one hand, and Elgar's *Gerontius*, Walton's *Belshazzar's Feast*, and Delius's *Sea-Drift*, on the other.

As always, progress results from making *demands*—demands upon the singer to respond to new ideas in vocal line and harmonic feeling. A choral singer today must be sensitive to the colour effects in the composer's thought, and this means that he must be blessed with powers of musicianship and technique hitherto quite uncalled for. But only when singers are endowed with absolute pitch will composers indeed be free to write for them as they do for instruments: their only limitation then will be the range imposed upon the voices by nature.

Whereas in much music of the past the *range* of voices has not been fully explored or exploited in *chorus* work, we find in modern scores sopranos and tenors frequently called upon to sing high B flat, and basses to scale the heights of top F sharp and descend to the depths of low D flat and C. Singers are in-

[1] Admittedly the memorization of a difficult interval or passage is an important factor in the expansion of vocal technique. By listening to such an interval or passage *played*, the singer increases his technical resource by the aid of impression and memory. Finally, this strengthens the power to feel such passages, and, therefore, to sing them as easily as more ordinary ones.

competent if not ready for wide intervals and unexpected harmonic progressions. Music abounds in consecutives of all kinds, pungent discordances both short- and long-lived, false relationships. Voices move in sweeping strands quite careless of the rules of the old continental theorists; composers write as though 'harmonic belief' (as Whittaker calls it) had not even *yet* entered their minds. This linear, rather than perpendicular, thinking creates clashes and piquancy which no system of harmony provides; from this point of view it may be fairly claimed that harmony, even in all its modern diversity, does not of itself yield *all* the colours of the musical spectrum.

Consider the following from Schütz's 'Sing to the Lord'. This passage shows us that even so far back in the past musicians were concerned about discordance as a means of expression, and *how to create it*.

Ex. 90

[*Transposed*]

The note D natural delayed in Tenor I appears in Soprano II. Mild as this effect may be, yet it is the kind of thing that even advanced students still hesitate to produce.

Ex. 91   Ibid

Note the clash between the first and second tenor parts on the second crotchet beat, creating expressive bitterness for a moment. There is more to notice in this bar if the student should look carefully around. Three hundred years have passed since Schütz exhibited these characteristics: yet is there a teaching-book which draws attention to such things; is there one which *encourages* a student to *use* them?

Let us see what Purcell did with regard to expressive dissonance; the following extract is the last six bars from his Anthem 'Hear my prayer'.

Examine in bars 1 and 2, *a–a* and *b–b*; in bar 3, ⌀ ⌀ ⌀; bars 3 and 4, *c–c*; bar 5 **–**.

These instances show how Purcell increased the expressiveness of his writing by the piquancy of his contrapuntal clashings. At *c–c* we see a case parallel to the Bach example, No. 27, p. 26, where consecutive octaves are hidden by the expedient of allowing the upper part to be prolonged as a suspension (in this case by Purcell it is an ornamental delaying) whilst the lower part moves to its note.

Ex. 92

72

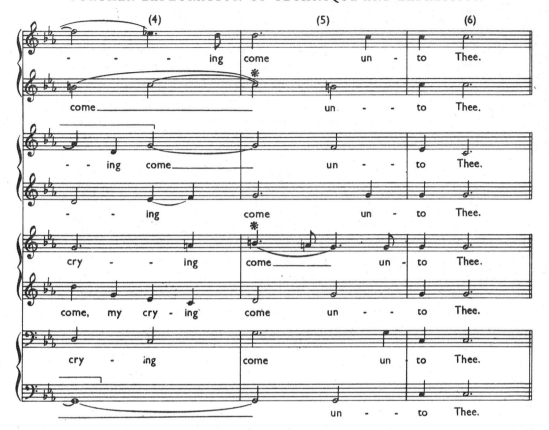

These, and the other means he employs for expressive purposes, are available to us today. The whole passage is adroitly handled and shows complexity of texture guided at every step by clarity of thought. The skill and attitude of mind revealed by the above indicate in some degree the stature of Purcell. There is little comparable to it, until, passing over the eighteenth and most of the nineteenth centuries, we come to Parry and Stanford, to be followed in due course by others, many of whom are still writing.

Read what Whittaker wrote on p. 116 of his *Collected Essays*:

'He [Purcell] seemed to be reaching out beyond the possibilities of his day, to some scheme of things unhampered by the limitations of music of the period. It is not a question of an occasional experiment, an exceptional progression now and again, but of a habitual mode of speech. . . . His texture, different in style from his immediate predecessors, is rich and unique. Like Bach, he incorporated into his style everything that he found satisfactory. . . . Like Bach, also, he added to the stores of harmonic resource enormously, and developed contrapuntal devices until the limit of that particular field of exploitation seemed to be reached. But, unlike Bach, *he has not fertilized the methods of succeeding composers*. . . . The fifteen years which elapsed between

73

Purcell's death and the arrival of Handel had witnessed a rapid change in musical outlook. . . . Purcell is peculiarly English and strangely insular; yet, though in the native-born music ever since his day we can trace the influence of every important foreign composer, there is practically never a suggestion of the one man who two and a half centuries ago spoke with such an authoritative and masterful voice.'

It is plain, indeed, that the serious-minded English student of music has much to browse over if he is to absorb his own national traditions. *It is for him to take away the reproach that 'Purcell has not fertilized the idioms and methods of composers'.*

No longer may the opinion be expressed that the ways and means shown in the technique of Byrd and Purcell be regarded as mere *period* characteristics. How can such a view be held when, as Whittaker says, 'Like Bach, Purcell incorporated into *his* style *everything that he found satisfactory*'? Like Bach, too, not only Purcell, but Palestrina, Byrd, and all the great ones did the same thing— they studied all they could lay their hands on and gathered up *everything they found satisfactory for their purposes, liturgical or humanistic.*

We have already seen Stanford, Parry, and Wood at work. Let us pass on to more modern examples, particularly of the English School.

Ex. 93

Ex. 94

The examples above are both from Peter Warlock's Carol, 'As dew in Aprylle', and surely suffice to represent the exquisite expression of one of the most sensitive musicians who ever lived.

The following excerpts are from two unaccompanied works by Herbert Howells. Ex. 95, 'Here is the little door', and Ex. 96, 'A Spotless Rose'.

Ex. 95

Those who have heard these know that their beauty lingers long in the mind; but alter a note of them, and they are spoiled.

The next example is by Gustav Holst and is taken from 'The Evening Watch'.

Holst was a master of technique and knew, with an uncanny surety, how to achieve his desired effects. In the above we see parallelism not in fifths, but in fourths and sevenths, the voices swaying in groups of three and four in contrary motion.

Now follow two short extracts from the *Mass in G minor* by Vaughan Williams.

Ex. 98

In these passages we see, used with superb mastery of effect, parallelism in fifths. Vaughan Williams recaptures the aloofness of medieval religious music.

Dr. Harold Darke in his *Communion Service in F* achieves sincerity of religious expression musically by a quiet mingling of voices whose smooth-flowing strands disdain neither consecutive fifths nor transient discordances.

Ex. 100

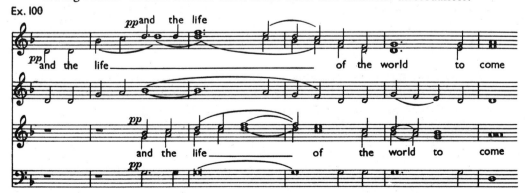

The next item is from the author's own work, *Stabat Mater Dolorosa*, which he begs leave to quote. In it is the endeavour to respond to the mystical spirit expressed in this thirteenth-century poem written by Jacopone da Todi. The bars given are those of the Amen which brings the work to a close.

Ex. 101

The following examples are taken from 'The Divine Image', the fifth of six Motets by E. J. Dent. The reader's attention is drawn to them on account of the remarkable contrapuntal chromaticism, which gives emphasis to the appeal of the text. The skill of the craftsman, in combining free and daring lines of vocal tone, is of the highest order.

Ex. 102

The extract that now follows is from the opening of a motet for double-choir unaccompanied, by J. A. Westrup.

This, like the motets by Dent, is of considerable dimension. In its daring dissonances, bold striding lines, and unexpected harmonic stresses, it seems to reveal kinship with the characteristics of Purcellian art, to which reference has been made.

As long ago as 1931 William Walton's *Belshazzar's Feast* appeared and was performed at the Leeds Musical Festival. The first entry of the voices—tenors and basses only—is indicative of the demands made upon choralists throughout the work.

Ex. 105

Such demands were met by the singers. On examination it will be found that, whatever the dissonance created by the parts *in combination*, the *individual* lines of tone consist of intervals that can be felt and anticipated mentally by the singer. This is not intended to suggest that passages are stripped of their difficulty; biting discordant elements can be annoying things to hold firmly against the rest of the chord. The work provides plenty of such instances, so that no further examples are called for here.

In the following passage from the same work there is modern contrapuntal fluidity revealing sure handling of texture; the voice parts seem to propel themselves along in curvilinear fashion as though it were Palestrina working with twentieth-century tools.

Ex. 106

Shall be found____ no more,____ no more,_____ no

Shall be found, shall____ be found____ no more,____ at all,____ no

Shall be found, shall____ be found____ no more,____ at all,____ no

Shall be found, shall__ be found no more at all, shall be found, no__

The next excerpt shows Walton expressing the poignancy of grief as the Israelites 'by the waters of Babylon sat down and wept'. The effects are not only harmonic: they are contrapuntal, too, and are such as should be carefully studied by all who are *stretching out* their expressive technique. It is important to note that each voice can feel its intervals; the trouble may be in *holding* them, but the demand may be stimulating and enjoyable with good choirs.

Ex. 107

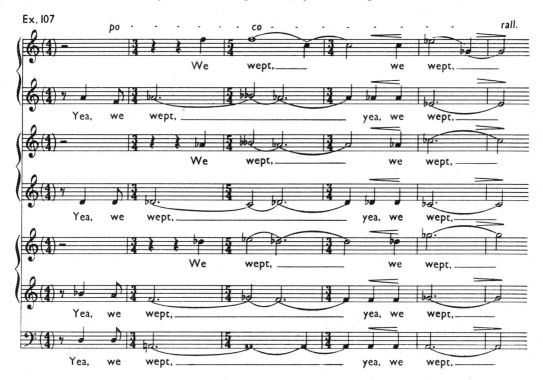

Many other quotations might be given from this work, but these must suffice. There are baritone solo passages, which, at first sight, might well daunt a singer; nevertheless, if carefully examined, the intervals will prove such as the trained musician should feel. Such passages make demands, but they are demands that can be met, although undoubtedly they represent considerable expansion of vocal technique.

Another work to which reference should be made is Thomas Wood's *Chanticleer*, written in 1947. It is an unaccompanied work which the composer describes as 'A Tale for Singing', the words being derived from 'The Nun's Priest's Tale' by Chaucer.

There is much freedom of tempo, particularly in recitative work, of which there is a good deal; the tempo changes from phrase to phrase and is obedient to the words. Humour there is in abundance, caught to the full by the music. Melodic lines, unfettered, create discordances as strident as they are apt. Voices are carried to their extremes of height and depth; in a word, technical resource seems to be exploited to an amazing extent, but controlled always by the consideration that singers should be able to feel and, therefore, sing their parts. It is impossible to give an impression of the versatility of the vocal writing by a mere quotation or two, but here are a few examples chosen at random which speak for themselves.

Ex. 108

Ex. 109

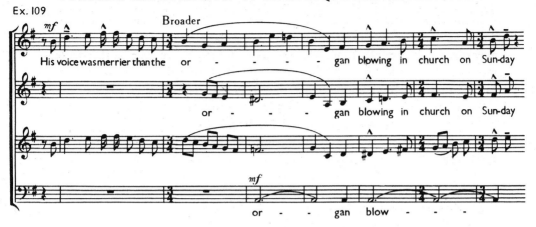

Ex. 110

This bar is repeated, making in all four bars
of this cock-crowing!

The last work from which quotation is to be made is 'Mater ora Filium', by
Sir Arnold Bax. The whole setting of this old carol should be most closely
studied, for it is a masterpiece of vocal orchestration as well as a superb example
of the handling of the resources afforded by double-choir. The effects can only
be realized by a choir of singing *musicians* as the passage which follows most
clearly reveals.

Ex. III (cont.)

Besides the works mentioned in these chapters are many others by contemporary English composers which claim their place as representative of the expansion of vocal technique and expression in all their variety. It is with great reluctance that examples from such works are omitted by reason of space, but it is hoped that students will not fail to make their own explorations in this field of peculiarly English art.

The point to be emphasized at the moment is not so much whether a composition appeals to our individual taste as whether it exemplifies true vocal expression which makes legitimate demands upon the singers. Above all, the parts *individually* should be such as can be *felt* and therefore *taken* by the performers whatever the combined effect of such parts may be. It is especially with this in mind that students should examine compositions in order to gather up 'whatever is satisfactory'.

It is interesting to see how far removed from the old continental theorists' views—views which held such dominating influence throughout the Classical Period—is the Contrapuntal Art of our own schools, not only of today but of Tudor times. These two schools are *outside the influence* of the major and minor key-system which characterized the Classical Period.

The controversy about the work of Corelli related on p. 65 is an indication of the grip in which theorists attempted to hold and control the art of musical composition. Evidently it needed the courage of an outstanding master like Corelli to flout their 'authority'.

It might be said, however, that the Corellian age, crowded with dilettanti, was different from ours; that no one nowadays heeds any 'authority' (if such indeed can be found). Nevertheless there is *one* authority which cannot be gainsaid, and that is the work of the recognized masters in the art of music. This book is nothing more than a consideration of what those masters have done. You can find in its pages quotation after quotation from their works. Any 'rules' and recommendations that you find here have been inferred from those works.

No composer ever lived who was not indebted to his forerunners. One writer[1] says of Brahms that he 'produced his works, not by ignoring what his predecessors had accomplished, but by adopting from them all that he believed sound and valuable, and organizing it for his own purpose. . . . Brahms created music based on what had gone before, but, nevertheless, essentially his own.'

Ralph Vaughan Williams sums up all this for us in a few words of wisdom which appear in his introduction to the book *England's Dances*.[2] He writes: 'It has been said that traditional art is an individual flowering on a common stem. By all means let us encourage the individual flowering, but one must not lose touch with the common stem.' If any should say 'why study technique at all?'

---

[1] *The Chamber Music of Johannes Brahms*, by Henry S. Drinker, Jnr.
[2] *England's Dances*——Douglas Kennedy.

the answer is that such study is our means of keeping touch with the common stem. True technique, order combined with freedom, is not based upon a set of rules arbitrarily imposed by the theorists, but upon accumulated wisdom of the *practical musicians*, the *makers* of music. We inherit what such men laboured to find out. Their legacy to us is a tradition which we may either treasure or ignore. Those who know it will treasure it; and they may confidently build upon it with the certainty that neither their originality nor their imagination will suffer injury.

COURSE OF STUDY

PART I

Sixteenth-century Style

I. SIX-PART WORK

As was stated in the introduction to this book, it is not intended to give specific attention to the idioms and idiosyncrasies of the style of Palestrina and others of the sixteenth century. Such attention would of itself require a separate book. Further, only passing observations concerning the modes are made. By the use of figured-bass some guidance has been provided towards the working of the exercises, and also food for thought—for those who can see in between the crevices.

The opening twenty-two bars of a six-part motet by Palestrina have been fully set down in order to give the reader an idea of the kind of thing Palestrina could create for six voice parts. The complete motet is eighty-nine bars long, and the first exercise (rather long) is taken from it. The leading musical ideas (commonly known as 'tags') have been indicated by numbers, thus drawing attention to their appearances and use. As was mentioned on p.12, it will be seen that the motet is a series of spans or periods in which *imitation of material* plays a great part.

Motet 'Susanna ab improbis' for six voices. Palestrina.

The tags are plainly indicated thus ——— and numbered; but it will be noticed that the parts are not wholly made up of this or that tag. There are places where the tag gives way and becomes a free part. It is hoped that sufficient indication *as to how Palestrina's mind set about its work* has been provided by the marking of such tags. This, the grasping of what Palestrina was doing, is the first important thing to lay hold on. Then, attention should be duly concentrated upon the free parts, or what some might call the filling-in parts. But they must not be merely fillers-in; *they must be in keeping with all that is going on.* The pursuit of this ideal cultivates in him both a sense of style and an ability for refined expression.

Often when a voice has had a rest, it will enter again with a tag, but this is not a necessity as is shown in bar 7 of the first soprano, and in bar 10 of the second soprano. They are free parts, doing a duty suitably.

In his study of the given twenty-two bars the reader will have noticed a number of things, but important among them will be that Palestrina *varies his method of using tags.* At the outset tag No. 1 is combined with a counter-tag

No. 2 in the alto. Then at bar 3, tag No. 1 appears in the second soprano. Against these, in bars 4, 5, and 6, the first soprano continues with 1a——, apparently a free part more or less, but important, as it is used again in bar 9 (Tenor I) and in bar 10 (Tenor II). Truly tags Nos. 1 and 1a form a long complete idea *repeated in full* in Tenor I and Tenor II when they enter at bars 6 and 8 respectively. A point worth mentioning here is the fact that when the second soprano begins in bar 3 with tag No. 1, it stops short of the full idea; that is, it does not sing No. 1a. Now students often ask, 'How far must a tag be carried on? Must it go its full length?' He will see the answer to his questions illustrated here. Obviously Palestrina let go of tag No. 1 in the second soprano to allow of the new entries which take place in bar 6. It is by grasping such points that the student learns the art which he sees so perfectly exemplified; he watches Palestrina's mind at work.

From bar 5, the three lower voices—Tenor I, II, and Bass—take up the opening bars as found in Soprano I, II, and Alto. Here, however, Palestrina allows the last voice, Tenor II, to complete the full version of tag No. 1 with 1a. Instead of stopping the Tenor II short (as he did Soprano II), he continues it and cleverly introduces two new tags, Nos. 3 and 4, against it. It is clear, therefore, why in the one instance he used tag No. 1, and in the other tag No. 1 plus 1a; into the bargain he avoids any sense of an important cadence and maintains continuity, a matter which should not be overlooked.

It will be noted that from bar 6 onwards, during which the three lower voices have the tag-work, the upper parts either rest or have free parts. (A composition cannot be made up of nothing but tags.) At bar 12 a touch of D minor is felt, but simultaneously two new tags (Nos. 3 and 4) appear, and thus maintain flow and continuity; there is no feeling of repose here.

Note should also be made regarding change of method in using the tags. At this point, bar 12, tags Nos. 3 and 4 come in together, other voices having free parts. Two bars later the second tenor and bass have these tags, going in pairs. There is then a single voice (second soprano) which has No. 3; but again Nos. 3 and 4 appear together in bars 15 and 16, and also in 17 and 18. Here is a definite cadence in G minor but no sense of stopping, for as before, a new tag No. 5 arrests attention. Thus we see the skill in preventing these 'spans' from marking out a composition into set blocks, as it were.

At bar 19 is seen another method of using tags. Here there is only one tag, not two as before, and it appears in five of the voices. Twice it happens in two voices simultaneously running in thirds, and once as an individual tag in the first soprano.

Thus far we have seen illustrated three different methods of using leading themes or tags. They should be well noted in the student's mind.

Such observations as have been made in our examination of these twenty-two bars should be remembered when working the following exercises. Imitation of a tag, it should be pointed out, is always open to slight adjustment. Sometimes a semibreve may appear as a minim; the interval between the opening notes may be altered, a third being answered by a second, and so on.

EXERCISE 1 (the last thirty bars of the above motet).

Complete the following. All rests are indicated and the first notes of tags shown. The basses are figured.

The ending denotes that the motet is in the third mode, transposed from the natural pitch of C to that of F, as indicated by the B flat in the signature. The student might well note the *keys* touched upon, by means of which Palestrina has given a little colouring. The word is used purposely, because, restricted as Palestrina's colouring obviously is, it is quite absurd to imagine that he was not conscious of its value. The idea that this music is just stone-grey and cold is utterly wrong. The colours are not of the vivid sort; how could they be? Most of them are familiar to us, perhaps too familiar; but with Palestrina they still retain their freshness. If anyone has doubt about Palestrina's sensitiveness to colour, let him study the *Stabat Mater*; also the Agnus Dei in his Mass *Æterna Christi Munera* where he will find the flattened seventh of the mode reserved for most tender expression.

The student will have observed that in the motet given above there is not a great deal of continuous six-part writing. Palestrina was doubtless aware of this. He knew how to make the most of his voices and therefore placed them carefully. The full choir of six parts generally appears near the end of all, or at the climax-periods where a sonorous effect (not necessarily loudness) is fitting. Surely it may be said that he *orchestrated* his vocal score. As an example of this let us examine briefly the treatment of the six voices (S^1, S^2, A, T^1, T^2, B) in the motet 'Haec dies quam fecit Dominus'. The first two bars are sustained chords (S^1, A, T^1, T^2) followed by four bars in imitative manner using the same voices; in bar 7 the Bass and Soprano II join in for a period of eight bars creating continuous six-part writing (apart from a minim rest in two places). This is most clearly a noble climax-point, with the fullest sonority from the voices. Then follow six bars of chordal work (the voices moving simultaneously note by note) for S^1, A, T^2, B, which are responded to by six bars for S^1, S^2, A, T^1. This antiphonal scoring recurs and winds up with fullness of tone by all six voice parts. An 'Alleluia' follows, twenty bars in length. It begins with close imitation of a pulsating motive taken up by four voices, then five, until during the last eight bars the full choir joins in, thus creating a fine climax.

EXERCISE 2. Complete the following. It is the opening of Palestrina's six-part Motet 'Haec dies quam fecit Dominus'. All rests are given. It is *freely* imitative, and the crotchet group of four becomes quite a feature:

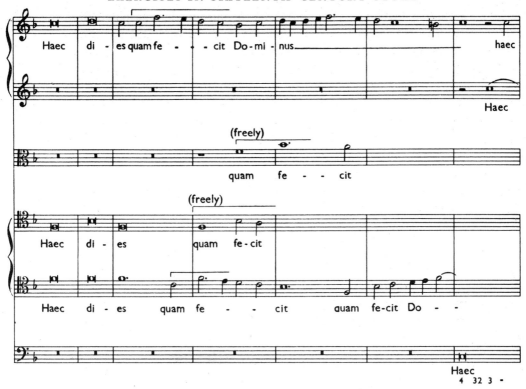

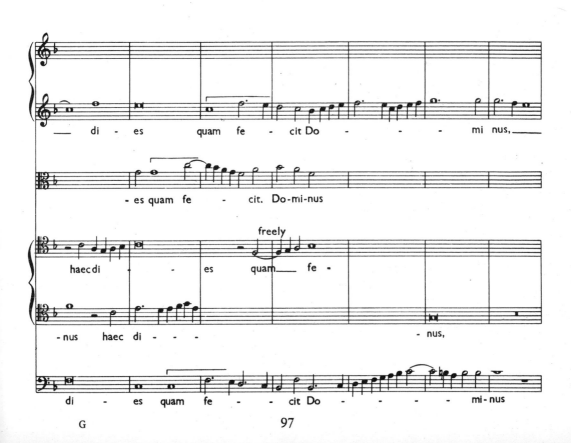

EXERCISE 3. Complete the following thirteen bars which are the ending of the Motet 'Haec dies'. The whole is built from one tag. The bass moves mostly in semibreves. The entry of tags and rests is indicated:

The above motet is clearly in the fifth mode.

EXERCISE 4. Complete the following. All rests are shown and all the entry points of the main tag (*a*) and subsidiary tag (*b*). The other parts are free:

EXERCISE 5. This exercise is for *five* voices; but only a skeleton framework is provided, giving the opening bars and rests. The words 'vidi te domine' are to be used.

EXERCISE 6. This, like the previous exercise, must be completed upon the skeleton sketch provided; but, unlike that exercise, it is for *six* voices.

II. DOUBLE-CHOIR WORK

Recalling the points which arose from our study of Palestrina's pure style of writing for double-choir, the student should complete the following exercises. Help is given by occasional figuring of the bass.

EXERCISE 7. Add the missing parts to the following excerpt from 'Jubilate Deo' by Palestrina. All rests are shown:

EXERCISE 8. The following exercise provides practice in responsive work, and moreover reveals harmonic aspects which should be carefully noted:

EXERCISE 9. From the Motet 'Surge, illuminare' (Palestrina). Complete the following bars. At (1) the third as leading-note occurs in both choirs: at (2) the first choir omits the third, and the second choir has it twice: at (3) in the first choir between soprano and tenor are consecutive octaves with a beat's rest separating them: at (4) between alto of the first choir and the tenor of the second choir are 'shadowing' octaves (see Ex. 77, p. 56):

EXERCISE 10. From 'Surge, illuminare' (Palestrina). Complete the following bars. At (1) in the second choir the leading-note is delayed by suspension in the soprano, and coincident with the resolution the leading-note appears in the tenor of the same choir (compare Ex. 57, p. 45).

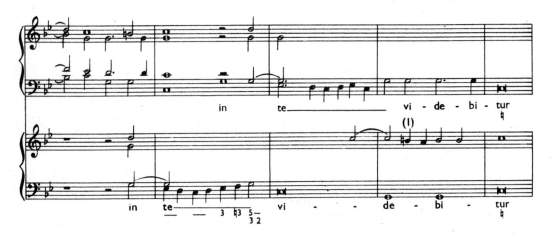

EXERCISE 11. Add a second choir to the given first choir. The bass of the second choir is indicated (from Palestrina's *Salve Regina*):

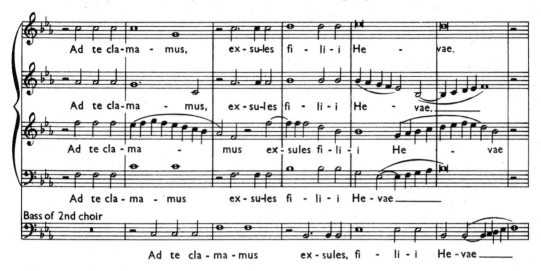

EXERCISE 12. Add a first choir to the given second choir. The bass of the *first* choir is given and figured (from Palestrina's *Salve Regina*):

EXERCISE 13. Add a first choir to the given second choir (from Palestrina's *Salve Regina*). Create an expressive tenor part; let the first choir enter at ★.

EXERCISE 14. Complete the following from Palestrina for double-choir. The parts move mostly note by note:

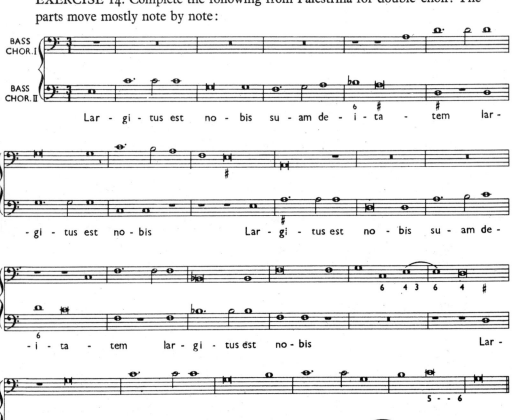

EXERCISE 15. Complete the following for double-choir from Palestrina's Motet 'Veni Sancte Spiritus'; the parts move quite simply in breves, semibreves, and occasional minims.

EXERCISES IN ORIGINAL COMPOSITION

EXERCISE 16. Using the scheme exemplified in 'Susanna ab improbis', p. 90 , set the following words for six voices.

Agnus Dei qui tollis peccata mundi
Dona nobis pacem.

EXERCISE 17. Making use of ideas gathered from the exercises already provided, set the following words for six voices as the ending of a motet:

'Exultemus et laetemur in ea.'

EXERCISE 18. Write a short six-part motet upon the words:

Nunc dimittis servum tuum Domine,
Secundum verbum tuum, in pace.

EXERCISE 19. Using the plan of Exercise 7, set the following words, closing with several bars for full *double-choir*:

Omnes gentes dicentes:
Gloria tibi Domine.

EXERCISE 20. Following the scheme of Exercise 11, set the following words for double-choir as the opening of a motet:

Ave Maria, gratia plena,
Dominus tecum.

EXERCISE 21. Taking Exercise 13 as your guide, set the following words for double-choir:

Domine Jesu Christe
Miserere mihi servo tuo.

EXERCISE 22. Using antiphonal overlapping phrases, and finally joining the choirs together, set the following for double-choir:

Gloria Patri, et Filio, et Spiritui Sancto,
Sicut erat in principio, et nunc et semper
Et in saecula saeculorum. Amen.

III. EIGHT-PART WORK

The following exercises are excerpts from Palestrina's writings. Although appearing notationally as two separate choirs, their treatment is that of a single choir of eight voices. The student is asked to complete them:

EXERCISE 23.

"Confitebor tibi, Domine"

EXERCISE 24.

"Notas facite in populis"

EXERCISE 25

"Domine, invirtute tua"

PART II

Post–Sixteenth-century Styles

REPRESENTATIVE OF TECHNIQUE OUTLINED IN CHAPTERS I–VII

In examination questions set as tests in six-part and eight-part writing, the student should not fall into five and seven parts by duplication unless the technique described on p. 21 is understood to be admissible.

The exercises which follow are of two kinds:

A. Those in which the student is intended to employ *foundational technique* in examination questions other than free composition (in which he is asked to create an original setting of given words).

This technique includes the points summarized on pp. 68–69, Chapters I–VI, and also the types of *delayed consecutives* mentioned in Chapter VII as follows:

> page 50, Ex. 66
>   „   50, Ex. 67, page 51, Exx. 68, 69
>   „   54, Ex. 74 (*b*)
>   „   57, Ex. 80 (*a*), (*b*), (*c*), (*d*)
>   „   58, Ex. 81
>   „   61, (*a*), (*b*), (*c*)
>   „   61, Ex. 84
>   „   64, Ex. 88

B. Those solely intended for free composition in which the student is at liberty to use the above foundational technique and all the relaxations discussed in Chapter VII (see summary on p. 69).

★   ★   ★

A. EXERCISES IN SIX-PART WORK

EXERCISE 26. Complete the following for S¹, S², A, T, B¹, B².

Notes: On the fourth crotchet at *A* the first bass begins the motive 'To all men be Thy Name'. Two other voices appear with this motive before Soprano I takes it up. After Soprano I has entered, the second bass sings the motive. On the second minim at *B* the three lowest voices enter with the motive 'Which is Love', the tune being in the tenor. This tune is imitated by A, S², and S¹ in turn. Parts may rest a little even when all the six voices are engaged. The piece ends with a Tierce de Picardie (E major).

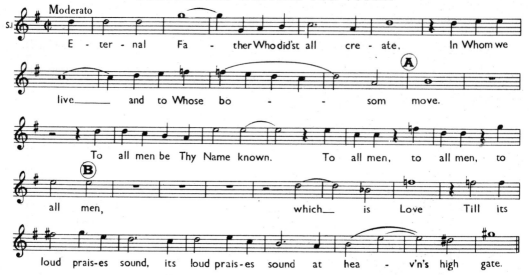

EXERCISE 27. The following shows a somewhat different build-up in treating the same words as Exercise 26. The three opening voices are responded to by another group of three, during which response the opening voices rest. However, they enter again with a new motive, which is taken up either in pairs or singly by all the voices, and continue together, creating full six-part writing to the end. The new entries dovetail, that is they should enter before the previous voices end their phrase.

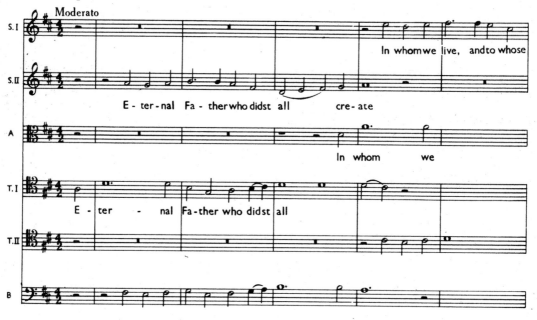

EXERCISE 28. Complete the following, which is similar in construction to Exercise 27. The Soprano I is given complete.

EXERCISE 29. Harmonize the following melody by adding flowing parts for S², A, T¹, T², B (six parts in all):

EXERCISE 30. Add 5 vocal parts above the following bass part:

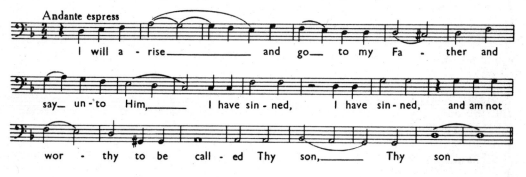

EXERCISE 31. To the following soprano part, add others for S², A, T¹, T², B:

EXERCISE 32. The following is taken from Charles Wood's *Magnificat and Nunc Dimittis in E major* for double-choir (A, T, B), published by The Year Book Press. Complete the missing parts. All rests are shown.

EXERCISE 33. Finding guidance from the plan of Exercise 26, set the following words for six voices:

> So when the last and dreadful hour
> This crumbling pageant shall devour,
> The trumpet shall be heard on high,
> The dead shall live, the living die,
> And music shall untune the sky.

EXERCISE 34. The following, from Charles Wood's Motet 'Haec dies', is given because it provides an example of the use of voices in interchangeable counterpoint. The opening three voices are used in changed positions in antiphonal fashion during the first sixteen bars, after which all six voices are engaged. The student is advised to procure a copy of this motet and study its construction and the resource which the composer brought into play. It is fifty-five bars in length.

Complete the given bars; all rests are shown:

EXERCISE 35. Starting as follows, complete the setting of the words for six voices, continuing with these words:

> Till all our strivings cease,
> Take from our souls the strain and stress
> And let our ordered lives confess
> The beauty of Thy peace.   *Whittier.*

EXERCISE 36. Complete this carol for six voices (S¹, S², A, T¹, T², B). The last eight bars or so should engage all the voices. Occasional extra parts such as occur in the opening bars may be added for effect, if desired:

> Love came down at Christmas,
> Love all lovely, Love Divine;
> Love was born at Christmas,
> Star and Angels gave the sign.   *Christina Rossetti.*

EXERCISES IN EIGHT-PART WORK

EXERCISE 37. Add seven parts for voices to this second bass part:

EXERCISE 38. Add seven parts for voices to this second bass part:

EXERCISE 39. Add seven parts for voices to the given second bass part:

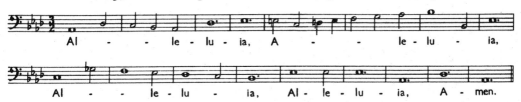

Al - - le - lu - ia, A - - le - lu - ia,

Al - - le - lu - ia, Al - le - lu - ia, A - men.

EXERCISE 40. Add seven parts for voices to this first soprano part:

Andante

EXERCISE 41. Add seven parts for voices to the following first soprano part. Insert the words:

Moderato

Let the peo-ple praise_____ Thee, O God: Yea,_ let all the peo - ple

praise Thee. Then shall the earth bring forth her in - crease_

_ and God_ shall give_ us_ His bless - ing.

EXERCISE 42. Add seven parts for voices to the following first soprano part. Insert the words:

EXERCISE 43. Harmonize for eight voices (the melody begins in C minor and ends in E flat major):

EXERCISE 44. Add seven parts to the following bass, treating it as the end of an eight-part motet:

EXERCISE 45. To this first soprano melody, add seven other voice parts:

EXERCISE 46. Add seven parts to this first soprano melody. Let all parts start together so that there is true eight-part writing throughout:

EXERCISE 47. Complete the following short motet for eight voices, of which the second bass is given:

A wise___ son,___ hear - eth his fa - ther's in - struc - tion, But a scor - ner hear - eth not re - buke,___ hear - eth not___ re - buke.

EXERCISE 48. Harmonize the following first soprano melody for an eight-part choir:

For sor - row, for sor - row, like a hea - vy - hang - ing bell once set a - ring - - - - - ing, by its own weight goes, by its own weight goes, goes, goes.___

EXERCISE 49. Set the following words, making a short eight-part song:

> With how sad steps, O Moon, thou climb'st the skies,
> How silently, and with how wan a face.
>
> *Sir Philip Sidney.*

EXERCISES IN DOUBLE-CHOIR WORK

EXERCISE 50. Writing for double-choir, complete the following. The last eight bars must show full eight-part writing:

EXERCISE 51. Complete the following for double-choir of eight voices. From the sixth bar real eight-part writing must be entirely (or almost entirely) maintained until the end:

EXERCISE 52. Complete the setting of the following words, for double-choir. Rests are shown. The continuation of the setting should involve both choirs in combination for several bars. Continue with the following words:

> For whoso findeth me, findeth life;
> But he that misseth me, wrongeth his own soul.

EXERCISE 53. Complete the following as for double-choir of eight voices:

Naught be all else to me,

Lord of my heart, Naught be all else to me, Naught be all

save that Thou art. Thou my best thought

else to me, save that Thou art. Thou my best

in the day and night, Wa - king or sleep -

thought in the day and night, Wa - king or

- ing, Thy pre - sence my light, my light.

sleep - ing, Thy pre - sence my light.

EXERCISE 54. Add six parts, making a complete double-choir exercise:

BASS
CHOIR I

BASS
CHOIR II

EXERCISE 55. Complete the following for double-choir (*Kitson*):

EXERCISE 56. Set the following words for double-choir as a short motet or anthem:

> If thine enemy be hungry, give him bread to eat;
> And if he be thirsty, give him water to drink:
> For thou shalt heap coals of fire upon his head,
> And the Lord shall reward thee.

A FEW ADDITIONAL EXERCISES

EXERCISE 57. Complete the following. All rests are shown:

R. Dering

EXERCISE 58. Complete the following. All rests are indicated:

R. DERING

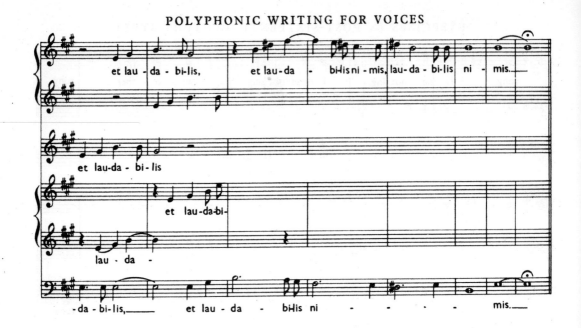

et lau - da - bi - lis, et lau - da - bi-lis ni - mis, lau - da - bi-lis ni - mis.__

et lau - da - bi - lis

et lau - da-bi-

lau - da -

-da - bi - lis,_____ et lau - da - bi-lis ni - - - - mis.__

EXERCISE 59. Complete the following. All rests are indicated:

I need not sing an - o - ther song, I need not sing an - o - ther

need not sing an - I need not

I need not sing__ an-o - ther song,

wrong, I need not sing an -

wrong, I need not sing an - o - ther song I need

wrong, I need not sing_____

EXERCISE 60. Complete the following. All rests are indicated:

EXERCISE 61. Set the following words for a double-choir of six male voices (A, T, B):

> I will not leave you comfortless:
> I will come to you.
> Peace I leave with you; my peace I give unto you.
> Let not your heart be troubled,
> Neither let it be afraid.

B. EXERCISES IN FREE COMPOSITION

EXERCISE 62. Set the following words for six-part choir:

> Fear no more the heat o' the sun,
>   Nor the furious winter's rages;
> Thou thy worldly task hast done,
>   Home art gone, and ta'en thy wages:
> Golden lads and girls all must,
> As chimney-sweepers, come to dust.
>   *Shakespeare.*

EXERCISE 63. Set the following for six-part choir:

> How happy is he born and taught
>> That serveth not another's will;
> Whose armour is his honest thought,
>> And simple truth his utmost skill!
>
> This man is freed from servile bands
>> Of hope to rise, or fear to fall;
> Lord of himself, though not of lands;
>> And having nothing, yet hath all.
>>>> *Sir Henry Wotton.*

EXERCISE 64. Set the following for six-part choir:

> I love the fitful gust that shakes
>> The casement all the day,
> And from the glossy elm tree takes
>> The faded leaves away,
> Twirling them by the window pane
>> With thousand others down the lane.
>>>> *John Clare.*

EXERCISE 65. Set the following for double-choir, A^1, T^1, B^1; A^2, T^2, B^2.

> Swiftly walk over the western wave,
>> Spirit of Night!
> Out of the misty eastern cave,
> Where, all the long and lone daylight,
> Thou wovest dreams of joy and fear,
> Which make thee terrible and dear,—
>> Swift be thy flight!
>>>> *Shelley.*

EXERCISE 66. Set the following for double-choir, A^1, T^1, B^1; A^2, A^2, T^2, B^2.

> Oh what can ail thee, knight-at-arms,
>> Alone and palely loitering?
> The sedge is wither'd from the lake,
>> And no birds sing.
>
> Oh, what can ail thee, knight-at-arms,
>> So haggard and so woebegone?
> The squirrel's granary is full,
>> And the harvest's done.
>>>> *Keats.*

133

EXERCISE 67. Set the following for double-choir, A^1, T^1, B^1; A^2, T^2, B^2.

> So the foemen have fired the gate, men of mine;
>> And the water is spent and gone?
> Then bring me a cup of the red Ahr-wine:
>> I never shall drink but this one.
>
> And reach me my harness, and saddle my horse,
>> And lead him me round to the door:
> He must take such a leap to-night perforce,
>> As horse never took before.
>
> They found him next morning below in the glen,
>> With never a bone in him whole—
> A mass or a prayer, now, good gentlemen,
>> For such a bold rider's soul!
>>> *Kingsley.*

EXERCISE 68. Set the following for eight-part choir, S^1, S^2, A^1, A^2, T^1, T^2, B^1, B^2.

> The splendour falls on castle walls
>> And snowy summits old in story:
> The long light shakes across the lakes,
>> And the wild cataract leaps in glory.
> Blow, bugle, blow, set the wild echoes flying,
> Blow, bugle; answer, echoes, dying, dying, dying.
>>> *Lord Tennyson.*

EXERCISE 69. Set the following for eight part-choir.

> The Assyrian came down like the wolf on the fold,
> And his cohorts were gleaming in purple and gold;
> And the sheen of their spears was like stars on the sea,
> When the blue wave rolls nightly on deep Galilee.
>
> Like the leaves of the forest when Summer is green,
> That host with their banners at sunset were seen:
> Like the leaves of the forest when Autumn hath blown,
> That host on the morrow lay wither'd and strown.
>>> *Lord Byron.*

EXERCISE 70. Set the following for eight-part choir.

On either side the river lie
Long fields of barley and of rye,
That clothe the wold and meet the sky;
And thro' the field the road runs by
To many-tower'd Camelot;
And up and down the people go,
Gazing where the lilies blow
Round an island there below,
The island of Shallot.

Lord Tennyson.

EXERCISE 71. Set the following for double-choir, S^1, A^1, T^1, B^1; S^2, A^2, T^2, B^2.

Sometimes a troop of damsels glad,
An abbot on an ambling pad,
Sometimes a curly shepherd-lad,
Or long-hair'd page in crimson clad,
Goes by to tower'd Camelot;
And sometimes thro' the mirror blue
The knights come riding two by two:
She hath no loyal knight and true,
The Lady of Shallot.

Lord Tennyson.

EXERCISE 72.

The wind was a torrent of darkness among the gusty trees,
The moon was a ghostly galleon tossed upon cloudy seas,
The road was a ribbon of moonlight over the purple moor,
And the highwayman came riding—
Riding—riding,—
The highwayman came riding, up to the old inn-door.

Alfred Noyes.

EXERCISE 73.

Full fathom five thy father lies;
Of his bones are coral made;
Those are pearls that were his eyes:
Nothing of him that doth fade,
But doth suffer a sea-change
Into something rich and strange.
Sea-nymphs hourly ring his knell:
Hark! now I hear them,—Ding-dong, bell.

Shakespeare.

EXERCISE 63. Set the following for six-part choir:

> How happy is he born and taught
> That serveth not another's will;
> Whose armour is his honest thought,
> And simple truth his utmost skill!
>
> This man is freed from servile bands
> Of hope to rise, or fear to fall;
> Lord of himself, though not of lands;
> And having nothing, yet hath all.
> *Sir Henry Wotton.*

EXERCISE 64. Set the following for six-part choir:

> I love the fitful gust that shakes
> The casement all the day,
> And from the glossy elm tree takes
> The faded leaves away,
> Twirling them by the window pane
> With thousand others down the lane.
> *John Clare.*

EXERCISE 65. Set the following for double-choir, A^1, T^1, B^1; A^2, T^2, B^2.

> Swiftly walk over the western wave,
> Spirit of Night!
> Out of the misty eastern cave,
> Where, all the long and lone daylight,
> Thou wovest dreams of joy and fear,
> Which make thee terrible and dear,—
> Swift be thy flight!
> *Shelley.*

EXERCISE 66. Set the following for double-choir, A^1, T^1, B^1; A^2, A^2, T^2, B^2.

> Oh what can ail thee, knight-at-arms,
> Alone and palely loitering?
> The sedge is wither'd from the lake,
> And no birds sing.
>
> Oh, what can ail thee, knight-at-arms,
> So haggard and so woebegone?
> The squirrel's granary is full,
> And the harvest's done.
> *Keats.*